SUPERSEDED

LEGAL NEGOTIATION

IN A NUTSHELL

SECOND EDITION

By

LARRY L. TEPLY
Professor of Law
Creighton University
and the
Werner Institute for Alternative
Dispute Resolution at
Creighton University

Mat #40264887

COPYRIGHT © 1992 WEST PUBLISHING CO.
© 2005 Thomson/West
     610 Opperman Drive
     P.O. Box 64526
     St. Paul, MN 55164–0526
     1–800–328–9352

Printed in the United States of America

ISBN 0–314–15417–5

TEXT IS PRINTED ON 10% POST
CONSUMER RECYCLED PAPER

To My Family—Frannie, Robert, Benjamin, Alison, Anna, and Nicholas Teply

*

PREFACE

Legal negotiation has become widely recognized as a subject of great importance in the practice of law. This work is designed to present a succinct treatment of legal negotiation to the reader. Because of size and format limitations of this series, difficult questions of exclusion and depth of treatment have constantly been presented in the preparation of this work. I have tried to balance the competing considerations and believe that the most important material has been included. This second edition, *inter alia*, substantially reorganizes the textual material; it adds discussion of several new topics; and it incorporates recent research on legal negotiation.

Because of the absence of footnoting in this series, I have not been able to provide full references to specific sources. Nonetheless, major sources have been indicated. By consulting the "Table of Cases," the "Table of Statutory, Procedural, Ethical, and Restatement Provisions," and the "References and Resources," the reader can follow up on the ideas and suggestions presented in the text. In addition to these directly acknowledged sources, I want to acknowledge ideas from numerous other sources of ideas that I have absorbed over years of teaching legal negotiation, but I have not directly attributed.

I want to acknowledge continuing permissions granted in conjunction with the first edition of this work. First and foremost, I want to thank Professor Gerald R. Williams and Thomson/West Group for their permission to make extensive use of copyrighted material from Professor Williams' *Legal Negotiation and Settlement*, Copyright © 1983 by West Publishing Company and his earlier *Effective Negotiation and Settlement*, Copyright © 1981 by Gerald R. Williams. Professor Williams' work represents an excellent pioneering effort from which lawyers and law students have gained much.

I want to thank Professor Carrie Menkel-Meadow and the *UCLA Law Review* for their permission to include quoted copyrighted material from Professor Menkel-Meadow's article *Toward Another View of Legal Negotiation: The Structure of Problem Solving*, 31 UCLA L. Rev. 754, 760, 801-02, 810 (1984), Copyright © 1984 by the *UCLA Law Review*, Los Angeles, California. I have also made reference to other helpful ideas and explanations in this article. Professor Menkel-Meadow's work provides a stimulating conceptualization of legal negotiation and would be profitable further reading.

Furthermore, I want to thank Professor Robert M. Bastress and Dean Joseph D. Harbaugh for granting me permission to use copyrighted material from their book, *Interviewing, Counseling, and Negotiating: Skills for Effective Representation*, Copyright © 1990 by Robert M. Bastress and Joseph D. Harbaugh. This book provides a useful presentation of interviewing, counseling, and negotiating skills and serves as an excellent and highly recommended text.

Finally, I would like to thank Shepard's/McGraw-Hill, Inc. for its past permission to quote copyrighted material from Richard A. Givens' book, *Advocacy: The Art of Pleading a Cause*, Copyright © 1980 by Shepard's/McGraw-Hill, Colorado Springs, Colorado. This book provides insights on the negotiation process from an advocacy perspective in an interesting and helpful manner.

With regard to the first edition of this work, I continue to thank the former Deans of Creighton Law School, Rodney Shkolnick and Lawrence Raful, for their past support. I also continue to recognize my outstanding student research assistants who reviewed drafts of the first edition: Angela Ballentine, Lisa Henkel, and Carolyn Sue DePriest Mouttet.

With regard to this second edition, I would like to acknowledge the support, assistance, and encouragement provided by my colleagues, students, and family. Particular mention should be made of my son, Robert Teply. As a lawyer and former editor of the *Harvard Negotiation Law Review*, Robert has provided many invaluable insights and suggestions. In addition, my son, Benjamin Teply, has provided expert help with the formulas and the technical, mathematical aspects of case evaluation.

I appreciate the efficient and cheerful secretarial assistance provide by Joan Hillhouse and Pat Anderson. In addition, I want to thank Kristina Schaefer, an outstanding student at Creighton Law School, for her excellent proofreading skills. I continue to thank our Law Library Director, Kay Andrus, and his staff for their excellent assistance. I also want to thank Professor Ed Morse for his helpful advice on the tax aspects of settlements.

Finally, I want to recognize the continuing research support provided by Creighton Law School. In particular, I want to recognize the leadership of Dean Patrick Borchers in developing the Werner Institute for Alternative Dispute Resolution here at Creighton Law School.

Larry L. Teply
Omaha, Nebraska
February 2005

OUTLINE

---

*

TABLE OF CASES

References are to Pages

———————

TABLE OF CASES

TABLE OF STATUTORY, PROCEDURAL, ETHICAL, AND RESTATEMENT PROVISIONS

FEDERAL

UNITED STATES CONSTITUTION

UNITED STATES CODE ANNOTATED

FEDERAL RULES OF CIVIL PROCEDURE

ETHICAL PROVISIONS

MODEL CODE OF PROFESSIONAL RESPONSIBILITY

MODEL RULES OF PROFESSIONAL CONDUCT

REFERENCES AND RESOURCES

Frank L. Acuff & Maurice Villere, *Games Negotiators Play*, BUS. HORIZONS, Feb. 1976.

AMERICAN BAR ASSOCIATION, MODEL CODE OF PROFESSIONAL RESPONSIBILITY (1981).

AMERICAN BAR ASSOCIATION, MODEL RULES OF PROFESSIONAL CONDUCT (1983).

7 AM. JUR. 2D *Attorneys at Law* §§ 172-175, 217-218, 227-232 (1997).

15A AM. JUR. 2D *Compromise and Settlement* §§ 6-34 (1976).

29 AM. JUR. 2D *Evidence* §§ 629-632 (1967).

51 AM. JUR. 2D *Limitation of Actions* §§ 389, 394 (2000).

ROBERT M. BASTRESS & JOSEPH D. HARBAUGH, INTERVIEWING, COUNSELING, AND NEGOTIATING: SKILLS FOR EFFECTIVE REPRESENTATION (1990).

MAX H. BAZERMAN & MARGARET A. NEALE, NEGOTIATING RATIONALLY (1992).

GARY BELLOW & BEA MOULTON, THE LAWYERING PROCESS: NEGOTIATION (1981).

DAVID A. BINDER ET AL., LAWYERS AS COUNSELORS: A CLIENT-CENTERED APPROACH (2d ed. 2004).

REFERENCES & RESOURCES

DAVID A. BINDER ET AL., LAWYERS AS COUNSELORS: A CLIENT-CENTERED APPROACH (1991).

DAVID A. BINDER & SUSAN PRICE, LEGAL INTERVIEWING AND COUNSELING: A CLIENT-CENTERED APPROACH (1977).

Wayne D. Brazil, *Protecting the Confidentiality of Settlement Negotiations,* 39 HASTINGS L.J. 955 (1988).

HERB COHEN, YOU CAN NEGOTIATE ANYTHING (1980).

Robert J. Condlin, *"Cases on Both Sides": Patterns of Argument in Legal Dispute-Negotiation,* 44 MD. L. REV. 65 (1985).

CHARLES B. CRAVER, EFFECTIVE LEGAL NEGOTIATION AND SETTLEMENT, 14 A.B.A. COURSE MATERIALS J. 7 (1989).

CHARLES B. CRAVER, EFFECTIVE LEGAL NEGOTIATION AND SETTLEMENT (5th ed. 2005).

DAN B. DOBBS, LAW OF TORTS (2000).

DAN B. DOBBS, HANDBOOK ON THE LAW OF REMEDIES: DAMAGES–EQUITY–RESTITUTION (2d ed. 1993).

JOHN PATRICK DOLAN, NEGOTIATE LIKE THE PROS (1992) (and Careertrack videotape).

HARRY T. EDWARDS & JAMES J. WHITE, THE LAWYER AS A NEGOTIATOR (1977).

Eunice A. Eichelberger, Annotation, *Authority of Attorney to Compromise Action—Modern Cases*, 90 A.L.R.4th 326 (1991).

Eunice A. Eichelberger, Annotation, *Ratification of Attorney's Unauthorized Compromise of Action*, 5 A.L.R.5th 56 (1993).

REFERENCES & RESOURCES

EXECUTIVE REPORTS CORP., WINNING BEFORE TRIAL: HOW
    TO PREPARE CASES FOR THE BEST SETTLEMENT OR TRIAL
    RESULT (1974).

Donald C. Farber, *Common-Sense Negotiation: How to Win
    Gracefully,* A.B.A.J., Aug. 1987, at 92.

ROGER FISHER & WILLIAM URY, GETTING TO YES: NEGOTIAT-
    ING AGREEMENT WITHOUT GIVING IN (1981).

Roger Fisher et al., *Negotiation Power: Ingredients in an
    Ability to Influence the Other Side*, in NEGOTIATION:
    STRATEGIES FOR MUTUAL GAIN 3-13 (Lavina Hall ed.,
    1993).

JAMES C. FREUND, SMART NEGOTIATING: HOW TO MAKE
    DEALS IN THE REAL WORLD (1992).

HARROP A. FREEMAN & HENRY WEIHOFEN, CLINICAL LAW
    TRAINING: INTERVIEWING AND COUNSELING 16 (1972).

Donald G. Gifford, *The Synthesis of Legal Counseling and
    Negotiation Models: Preserving Client-Centered Advo-
    cacy in the Negotiation Context,* 34 UCLA L. REV. 811
    (1987).

DONALD G. GIFFORD, LEGAL NEGOTIATION: THEORY AND
    APPLICATIONS (1989).

RICHARD A. GIVENS, ADVOCACY: THE ART OF PLEADING A
    CAUSE (2d ed. 1985).

RICHARD A. GIVENS, ADVOCACY: THE ART OF PLEADING A
    CAUSE (3d ed. 1992).

ALVIN L. GOLDMAN, SETTLING FOR MORE: MASTERING
    NEGOTIATING STRATEGIES AND TECHNIQUES (1991).

REFERENCES & RESOURCES

Thomas F. Guernsey, *Truthfulness in Negotiation,* 17 U. RICH. L. REV. 99 (1982).

THOMAS F. GUERNSEY, A PRACTICAL GUIDE TO NEGOTIATION (1996).

ROGER S. HAYDOCK, NEGOTIATION PRACTICE (1984).

Geoffrey C. Hazard, Jr., *The Lawyer's Obligation to Be Trustworthy When Dealing With Opposing Parties,* 33 S.C. L. REV. 181 (1981).

G. NICHOLAS HERMAN ET AL., LEGAL COUNSELING AND NEGOTIATION: A PRACTICAL APPROACH (2001)

Norbert Jacker, *Negotiation Techniques for the Trial Advocate* (1983) (videotape).

CHESTER L. KARRASS, GIVE & TAKE: THE COMPLETE GUIDE TO NEGOTIATING STRATEGIES AND TACTICS (rev. ed. 1993).

CHESTER L. KARRASS, "IN BUSINESS AS IN LIFE—YOU DON'T GET WHAT YOU DESERVE, YOU GET WHAT YOU NEGO-TIATE" (1996).

CHESTER L. KARRASS, THE NEGOTIATING GAME: HOW TO GET WHAT YOU WANT (rev. ed. 1992).

ROBERT E. KEETON, INSURANCE LAW § 7.8 (1971).

W. PAGE KEETON ET AL., PROSSER & KEETON ON TORTS (5th ed. 1984).

A.E. Korpela, Annotation, *Admissibility of Admissions Made in Connection with Offers or Discussions of Compromise,* 15 A.L.R.3D 13 (1967).

REFERENCES & RESOURCES

WAYNE R. LAFAVE & AUSTIN W. SCOTT, JR., CRIMINAL LAW (2d ed. 1986).

WAYNE R. LAFAVE, CRIMINAL LAW (4th ed. 2003).

DAVID A. LAX & JAMES K. SEBENIUS, THE MANAGER AS NEGOTIATOR: BARGAINING FOR COOPERATION AND COMPETITIVE GAIN (1986).

Legal Malpractice–Attorney's Unreasonable Settlement or Failure to Settle Client's Case, 26 AM. JUR. PROOF OF FACTS 2D 703 (1981).

ROY J. LEWICKI ET AL., NEGOTIATION: READING, EXERCISES, AND CASES (3d ed. 1999).

DAVID V. LEWIS, POWER NEGOTIATING TACTICS AND TECHNIQUES (1981).

Gary T. Lowenthal, *A General Theory of Negotiation Process, Strategy and Behavior,* 31 U. KAN. L. REV. 69 (1982).

Susan R. Martyn, *Informed Consent in the Practice of Law,* 48 GEO. WASH. L. REV. 307 (1980).

Suzanne J. McKinley & Carol A. Gosselink, *What You Don't Say Says It All,* COMMUNICATOR'S J., May/June 1983.

MICHAEL MELTSNER & PHILLIP G. SCHRAG, PUBLIC INTEREST ADVOCACY: MATERIALS FOR CLINICAL LEGAL EDUCATION (1974).

Carrie Menkel-Meadow, *Toward Another View of Legal Negotiation: The Structure of Problem Solving,* 31 UCLA L. REV. 754 (1984).

REFERENCES & RESOURCES

ROBERT H. MNOOKIN ET AL., BEYOND WINNING: NEGOTIAT-
ING TO CREATE VALUE IN DEALS AND DISPUTES (2000).

GERALD I. NIERENBERG, FUNDAMENTALS OF NEGOTIATING
(1973).

GERALD I. NIERENBERG, THE COMPLETE NEGOTIATOR (1986).

Gerald I. Nierenberg & Henry H. Calero, *Meta-Talk: The
Art of Deciphering Everyday Conversation,* MBA MAG.,
Jan. 1984.

Eleanor Norton, *Bargaining and The Ethic of Process,* 64
N.Y.U. L. REV. 493 (1989).

Rex. R. Perschbacher, *Regulating Lawyers' Negotiations,* 27
ARIZ. L. REV. 75 (1985).

PERSONAL INJURY VALUATION HANDBOOKS (LRP Publications).

Geoffrey M. Peters, *The Use of Lies in Negotiation,* 48 OHIO
ST. L.J. 1 (1987).

DEAN G. PRUITT, NEGOTIATION BEHAVIOR (1981).

DEAN G. PRUITT & JEFFREY Z. RUBIN, SOCIAL CONFLICT:
ESCALATION, STALEMATE AND SETTLEMENT (2d ed.
1993).

HOWARD RAIFFA, THE ART AND SCIENCE OF NEGOTIATION
(1982).

James L. Regelhaupt, Jr., Annotation, *Legal Malpractice in
Settling or Failing to Settle Client's Case,* 87 A.L.R.3D
168 (1978).

Alvin B. Rubin, *A Causerie on Lawyers' Ethics in Negotiation,* 35 LA. L. REV. 577 (1975).

REFERENCES & RESOURCES

JEFFREY Z. RUBIN & BERT R. BROWN, THE SOCIAL PSYCHOL-
OGY OF BARGAINING AND NEGOTIATION (1975).

TOM RUSK, THE POWER OF ETHICAL PERSUASION: FROM
CONFLICT TO PARTNERSHIP AT WORK IN PRIVATE LIFE
(1993).

Gregory G. Sarno, Annotation, *Adequacy of Defense Counsel's Representation of Criminal Client Regarding Plea
Bargaining,* 8 A.L.R.4TH 660 (1981).

MARK K. SCHOENFIELD & RICK M. SCHOENFIELD, LEGAL
NEGOTIATIONS: GETTING MAXIMUM RESULTS (1988).

NANCY L. SCHULTZ & LOUIS J. SIRICO, JR., LEGAL WRITING
AND OTHER LAWYERING SKILLS (4th ed. 2004).

Richard Shell, *Opportunism and Trust in the Negotiation
of Commercial Contracts: Toward a New Cause of
Action,* 44 VAND. L. REV. 221 (1991).

G. RICHARD SHELL, BARGAINING FOR ADVANTAGE: NEGOTIA-
TION STRATEGIES FOR REASONABLE PEOPLE (1999).

JOSEPH SINDELL & DAVID SINDELL, LET'S TALK SETTLEMENT
(1963).

DONALD B. SPARKS, THE DYNAMICS OF EFFECTIVE NEGOTIA-
TION (1982).

Mark Spiegel, *Lawyering and Client Decision Making:
Informed Consent and the Legal Profession*, 128 U. PA.
L. REV. 41 (1979).

Robert S. Summers, *"Good Faith" in General Contract Law
and the Sale Provisions of the Uniform Commercial
Code,* 54 VA. L. REV. 195 (1968).

REFERENCES & RESOURCES

DIANA TRIBE, NEGOTIATION (1993).

David M. Trubeck et al., *The Costs of Ordinary Litigation*, 31 UCLA L. REV. 72 (1983).

WILLIAM URY, GETTING PAST NO: NEGOTIATING WITH DIFFICULT PEOPLE (1991).

Video Arts, *From "No" to "Yes": The Constructive Route to Agreement* (1988) (videotape).

JACK B. WEINSTEIN ET AL., WEINSTEIN'S EVIDENCE Rule 408, 409, 410 (1996).

James J. White, *Machiavelli and the Bar: Ethical Limitations on Lying in Negotiation*, 1980 AM. B. FOUND. RES. J. 926.

Gerald R. Williams, *Negotiation as a Healing Process*, 1996 J. DISPUTE RES. 1.

Gerald R. Williams, *Style and Effectiveness in Negotiation*, in NEGOTIATION: STRATEGIES FOR MUTUAL GAIN 151-74 (Lavina Hall ed., 1993).

GERALD R. WILLIAMS, LEGAL NEGOTIATION AND SETTLEMENT (1983).

GERALD R. WILLIAMS, EFFECTIVE NEGOTIATION AND SETTLEMENT (1981).

CHARLES W. WOLFRAM, MODERN LEGAL ETHICS (1986).

7B CHARLES A. WRIGHT ET AL., FEDERAL PRACTICE AND PROCEDURE: CIVIL 2D §§ 1797, 1797.1 (2d ed. 1986).

BOB WOOLF, FRIENDLY PERSUASION: MY LIFE AS A NEGOTIATOR (1990).

LEGAL
NEGOTIATION

IN A NUTSHELL

SECOND EDITION

*

CHAPTER 1

NEGOTIATION IN LAW PRACTICE

A. INTRODUCTION

Negotiation is an integral part of the lives of many professionals, especially lawyers. In fact, negotiation is often described as a lawyer's principal occupation. Lawyers use negotiation *to create legal relationships* for their clients, such as partnerships, corporations, franchises, and joint ventures. They use negotiation *to effect transactions* for their clients, including real estate deals, commercial sales, corporate mergers, and employment agreements. They also use negotiation *to resolve legal disputes* for their clients—with or without resort to litigation. For example, in many business contexts, lawyers try to work out misunderstandings and disputes through discussion and compromise to avoid the strains that litigation creates on the relationship between the parties.

Even when a legal dispute results in litigation, a settlement is negotiated prior to trial in a high percentage of cases in both state and federal courts. For example, of the total civil cases filed in federal district courts (excluding land condemnation cases) in recent years, only about 5% reached trial. The remaining 95% were terminated without trial—in most instances, by negotiated settlement agreements.

1

On an individual level, an empirical study published in the *UCLA Law Review* found that lawyers devoted an average of 15.1% of their time to settlement discussions. This percentage was exceeded only by the time spent in discovery activities (16.7%) and the time spent conferring with the client (16%). The remaining time was spent in the following activities: pleadings (14.3%), factual investigation (12.8%), legal research (10.1%), hearings and trials (8.6%), appeals and enforcement (0.9%), and other (5.5%).

The importance of negotiation in law practice is further highlighted by the benefits of negotiated settlements of legal disputes from a client's perspective:

(1) A negotiated settlement avoids the uncertainties and vagaries of trial and appeal—settling for what is certain over what is far from certain;

(2) A negotiated settlement avoids the economic costs of trial—including delays associated with trial, court costs, expert witness fees, additional discovery, time lost by the parties in preparing for and attending trial, and additional legal fees;

(3) A negotiated settlement avoids social and psychological costs of trial—including anxiety and stress of trial, possible embarrassment or adverse publicity, and further damage to the relationship between the parties;

(4) A negotiated settlement avoids the "winner-take-all" nature of most legal remedies;

(5) A negotiated settlement avoids the limited scope of the remedies available in court—providing an

opportunity to fashion a broader package in the best interests of both parties;

(6) A negotiated settlement avoids the risk of unfavorable interpretations of the law; and

(7) A negotiated settlement avoids the possibility of harmful admissions or findings of fact that could be used against clients in related litigation (issue preclusion).

Negotiation of legal disputes also has broader significance. From an institutional perspective, negotiated settlements reduce the workload placed on the judicial system. Because of negotiated settlements, both the trial and appellate courts have more time to consider cases that require trial and appellate review. From an individual lawyer's perspective, negotiated settlements increase the number of cases that a lawyer can process in a practice. From a psychological and anthropological perspective, negotiated settlements facilitate the "healing process." As well described by Professor Gerald Williams, the process of negotiation itself helps the parties not only settle the immediate conflict, but also provides the potential for the parties to resolve underlying social and psychological issues in a positive way.

Compromise is a critical element in the legal negotiation process. In a legal negotiation, the parties involved engage in discussion and exchange to reconcile the possibly competing or conflicting interests. The purpose of this interchange is to reach an acceptable voluntary solution or agreement among the parties. The willingness to reach such a solution or agreement is strongly influenced by two divergent factors: (1) *restraints* on the parties, including concern over possible losses if an agreement is not reached, the possible lack of trustworthiness of the other parties, and social pressures; and (2) *drives* toward agreement, including the possible benefits from agreement and the desire to be cooperative.

Another critical element in the negotiation process is *meaningful communication*. Such communication facilitates the reaching of a mutually acceptable agreement. Traditionally, this process has called for the parties to submit offers, consider arguments, and make counteroffers. Still another basic element in this process is a willingness to *compromise*, thus avoiding the risks of impasse and securing the benefits of an agreement— such as a mutually agreeable exchange of desired property, services, or money— without resort to physical force, legal action, or other means of handling the matter. This process may also involve discovering and evaluating the various alternatives in light of the parties' interests to create a solution that yields maximum benefit to both sides.

Some individuals are uncomfortable with the legal negotiation process because concession making and compromising involve a certain amount of argument, haggling, and stress. Furthermore, in certain contexts, some individuals are uncomfortable with compromising; they consider it an unprincipled "selling out."

Other individuals are uncomfortable with negotiation because it involves risks. For example, negotiators can be duped into conceding much more than necessary to reach an agreement. In addition, after an agreement has been reached and one side has performed, a risk exists that the other side will refuse to perform its part of the bargain. Much of being a successful negotiator depends on learning when and how to compromise in the face of these risks. Another part of negotiating draws on the negotiator's ability to create alternative solutions to satisfy a party's needs.

Negotiating in a legal context is a difficult and challenging task for several reasons. In the real world of legal disputes—unlike in economic and game-theory models of negotiation that assume complete or perfect knowledge of all information—legal negotiators must often make recommendations to their clients without being certain the negotiators know all the relevant information. For example, one or both sides may overlook crucial evidence or information. Legal negotiators similarly face the real risk that new information—favorable or unfavorable—may be discovered at any time or that new legal developments—again favorable or unfavorable—may occur.

Another reason why negotiation in a legal context is difficult and challenging relates to evaluation and prediction. The baseline for evaluation of most lawsuits is the probable trial outcome. What, if anything, a judge or jury might award at trial in a particular case is often subject to genuine dispute. Lawsuits involve a variety of intangibles, ranging from the amount that a jury might award for pain and suffering to uncertainties whether any liability exists at all. The varying views of the trial-advocacy skills of the lawyers involved compound the uncertainties caused by these intangibles.

Legal negotiation is further complicated by a lack of knowledge about how opposing parties and their lawyers will act and, more importantly, react in a legal negotiation context. Economic and game-theory models of negotiation assume that the negotiators will make decisions on the basis of rational choice. Legal negotiators, however, must deal with clients and opposing parties who may refuse to move from unreasonable positions and who may make apparently irrational decisions.

Economic and game-theory models of negotiation also assume that both parties know the importance of each item in the "payoff matrix." Yet legal negotiators often must guess at the value of a particular item to the opposing party. For example, a negotiator will seldom know exactly how important preventing adverse publicity or avoiding setting an adverse precedent is to the opposing party. This lack of knowledge again adds to the difficulty of negotiating in a legal context.

B. IMPORTANCE OF LEARNING AND PERFECTING NEGOTIATION SKILLS

As discussed in detail in the next section, negotiating skills are a significant part of representing a client well. In extreme circumstances, poor negotiating skills may give rise to a legal malpractice claim. Negotiating skills are also an important element in a lawyer's reputation. Because of the significant role of negotiation in law practice and the difficulties and challenges legal negotiators face, a high priority on learning and perfecting legal negotiation skills is justified.

C. REPRESENTING CLIENTS IN LEGAL NEGOTIATIONS

One of the distinguishing characteristics of legal negotiation is that lawyers ordinarily represent clients, not themselves. The existence of this professional relationship between lawyer and client has important consequences. First, this relationship imposes ethical responsibilities on lawyers. Second, it creates the risk of malpractice claims based on the lawyer's conduct related to legal negotiations. Third, the professional relationship between lawyer and client complicates the decision-making process because legal negotiators must deal not only with the opposing counsel and the opposing party but also with their own clients. For example, lawyers and their clients may have serious disagreements about the negotiating strategy and style that should be adopted or the desirability of accepting an offer that has been made by the other side. Furthermore, conflicts may arise when the lawyer's interests are not sufficiently aligned with those of the client.

1. THE OBLIGATION OF COMPETENT REPRESENTATION

Lawyers are obligated to represent their clients competently in legal negotiation. This obligation emanates from two sources: (1) the rules of professional responsibility governing lawyers; and (2) the law itself in the form of a legal malpractice standard. Assessing whether a particular lawyer has met this obligation of competent representation, however, is not an easy task.

a. Professional Ethical Rules

Rule 1.1 of the American Bar Association's *Model Rules of Professional Conduct* (1983) (hereafter referred to as the "ABA's *Model Rules*") states that "[a] lawyer shall provide competent representation to a client. Competent representation requires the legal knowledge, skill, thoroughness and preparation reasonably necessary for the representation." In a negotiation context, the directives of this ethical rule that need to be emphasized are *thoroughness* and *preparation*. As discussed in the next chapter, being prepared is one of the principal shared characteristics of legal negotiators who are viewed as effective. Thorough preparation allows legal negotiators to demonstrate the strength of their client's position and interests convincingly and persistently. It also allows legal negotiators to deal with weaknesses as effectively as possible.

b. Assessing Negotiating Competence or Effectiveness

The professional ethical standard requires competence in negotiation. One problem in assessing legal negotiators' professional competence, however, is the lack of consensus about what exactly should be deemed competent or effective. One way of assessing negotiating competence or effectiveness is to focus on the *outcome*. Is it obtaining the highest (or, correspondingly, the lowest) possible amounts in settlement? Is it achieving "fair results" for everyone concerned? Is it achieving settlements that order the available economic resources in the "most efficient" way? Is it achieving settlements that best benefit the legal system and society as a whole? Is it reaching "principled" agreements that meet "objective criteria" of fairness? Is it reaching agreements that consider all relevant information and arguments, not just those that support one side?

Another way of assessing negotiating competence or effectiveness is to focus on the *process*. Is it negotiating in a way that most efficiently uses the available resources, including cost-reducing procedures, communication channels, case-management techniques, and judicial resources? Is it negotiating in a way that avoids using tactics that unnecessarily increase the costs to one or both of the parties? Is it negotiating in a way that reduces the costs of the negotiation in terms of time, money, and psychological harm?

With respect to the outcome measures of effectiveness, the American Bar Association's *Model Code of Professional Responsibility* (1981) (hereafter referred to as the "ABA's *Model Code*") (still used for professional discipline in some jurisdictions) and the ABA's current *Model Rules* (adopted in a majority of jurisdictions) leave the questions posed above largely unanswered. Indeed, support for both a profit-maximizing and a fair-to-all standard can be found in both the

Model Code and the *Model Rules*. Similarly, the bar and legal commentators are divided about which view is the proper or best standard. Generally speaking, maximizing settlement is widely regarded as a common goal among legal negotiators who are viewed by their peers as effective negotiators. Although it may often be inconsistent with maximizing settlement, getting a fair (reasonable) settlement is also seen as the appropriate goal by many effective legal negotiators.

c. *Legal Malpractice*

An essential part of the lawyer-client relationship is that a lawyer must faithfully, honestly, and consistently represent the interests and protect the rights of the client. When negotiating on a client's behalf or advising a client about settlement, a lawyer is held to the general standards used to judge a lawyer's conduct in all malpractice actions: the lawyer must exercise the knowledge, skill, and ability ordinarily possessed and exercised under similar circumstances by other lawyers in the community.

On occasion, lawyers have been held liable for malpractice for failing to meet this standard in a negotiation context. In a Massachusetts case, for example, a lawyer was retained to represent a bicyclist who had been seriously injured when a car traveling in the same direction struck the bicyclist at the edge of the road. The bicyclist was wearing dark clothing, and the bicycle may have lacked proper reflectors. The bicyclist's lawyer was a part-time solo practitioner who had not tried a case for several years and who mainly handled real estate conveyancing. The lawyer delayed in filing suit until sixteen months after the accident. For no apparent reason, the lawyer did not obtain service on the driver defendant for more than ten months after filing the complaint. The lawyer did not examine the motor vehicle and did not engage in any productive pretrial discovery. The lawyer failed to learn that shortly after the accident, the driver stated that the driver neither saw the bicyclist nor the bicycle before the driver's vehicle struck them. Instead, the lawyer relied on information volunteered by the driver's insurer.

Two months before the trial date, the lawyer consulted an experienced personal injury litigator about referring the case. The case was not referred, however, because the lawyer would not agree to an even division of the one-third contingent fee. At that point, the lawyer made a settlement demand of $250,000 on the driver's insurer. The lawyer was unaware of the available insurance coverage, but told the client that only $250,000 was available—when, in fact, $1,000,000 was. The driver's insurer made various offers of settlement, each of which the lawyer recommended that the client accept. The client, however, refused. Finally, shortly before trial, after the lawyer told the client that the case could not be won if the case went to trial, the client agreed to settle the personal injury claim for $160,000.

In the malpractice action, *Fishman v. Brooks* (1986), the jury found that (1) the lawyer had negligently handled the personal injury action; (2) the lawyer had negligently recommended that the client accept an unreasonable settlement offer; and (3) the client would have obtained a better result had the lawyer exercised adequate skill and care. Based on these findings, the jury found that the client had been damaged as a result of the lawyer's negligence in the amount of $525,000.

2. PROFESSIONAL OBLIGATION TO KEEP CLIENTS INFORMED

Information is an essential prerequisite to informed decision making by clients about their cases. Rule 1.4 of the ABA's *Model Rules* specifically requires lawyers to keep clients "reasonably informed about the status of a matter [and] promptly comply with reasonable requests for information" and to "explain a matter to the extent reasonably necessary to permit [clients] to make informed decisions regarding the representation." Rule 1.4 does not have a direct counterpart in the disciplinary rules of the ABA's *Model Code*, but it is supported by statements in ethical considerations. For example, Ethical Consideration 7-8 provides that "lawyer[s] should exert [their] best efforts to insure that decisions of [their] client[s] are made only after [their clients have] been informed of relevant considerations." Rule 3-500 of the California Rules of Professional Conduct requires that a client be kept "reasonably informed about significant developments relating to the employment or representation . . . ." Rule 3-500 also imposes the duty to "promptly comply with reasonable requests for information."

Thus, lawyers have the obligation to help their clients understand the steps of the litigation process—commencement, discovery, trial, and appeal. Clients should be told about the legal theories and defenses involved in their cases. Likewise, clients should be made aware of any potential defenses, problems of proof or credibility, and other weaknesses. As part of good case management and client counseling, clients should be kept informed about the progress of their cases and they should be routinely sent copies of all documents—with cover letters explaining their significance.

One problem that lawyers face in keeping clients informed and in advising them about probable trial outcomes or settlement sometimes is a result of the initial evaluations that lawyers give to their clients. Clients often ask lawyers to estimate what cases are worth. Some lawyers—in order to secure the "business"—have the tendency to make overly optimistic estimates. These estimates may result in unrealistic expectations on the part of clients. When these expectations are left unmodified by a lawyer's failure to keep the client informed and to provide updated evaluations of the strengths and weaknesses of the case, serious disagreements may arise.

Typically, this problem comes to a head when the lawyer recommends a settlement that differs significantly from the client's expectations. This reason may account for a significant number of cases needlessly going to trial. For example, in a study of litigation in

Phoenix, Arizona, by Professor Gerald Williams, over 50% of the cases that went to trial did so because one or both of the clients were unwilling to accept their *own* lawyer's recommendation to settle.

③ INFORMED CLIENT DECISION MAKING AND CONSENT

Central to the settlement process in a legal context is the informed decision making and consent of the client. It is the client's case, not the lawyer's. Rule 1.2 of the ABA's *Model Rules* provides that lawyers must abide by clients' decisions about "the objectives of representation"—within the limits imposed by law and the lawyer's professional obligations. With regard to legal negotiation, Rule 1.2(a) specifically states that "[a] lawyer shall abide by a client's decision whether to settle a matter." Thus, in *Rogers v. Robson, Masters, Ryan, Brumund & Belom* (1980), the lawyers who had been retained by a physician's malpractice insurer were held liable for damages suffered by the physician when the lawyers settled the action without the physician's consent and contrary to the physician's express instructions. The lawyers' duty to disclose the insurer's intent to settle the litigation stemmed from the lawyer-client relationship and was not affected by the extent of the insurer's authority to settle the case without the physician's consent.

Rule 1.2(a) has no direct counterpart in Disciplinary Rules of the ABA's *Model Code*, but it is supported by several statements of ethical considerations. For example, Ethical Consideration 7-7 states that "[i]n certain areas of legal representation not affecting the merits of the cause or substantially prejudicing the rights of a client, [lawyers are] entitled to make decisions on [their] own. But otherwise, the authority to make decisions is exclusively that of the client."

By placing the ultimate responsibility for decision making on the client, the ethical rules provide the key to resolving some of the conflicts between an individual client's interests and broader social goals. For example, the decision to seek clarifications or changes in the law through trial and appeal may conflict with the client's immediate interest. Indeed, the opposing party may be willing to pay a premium to settle a case to avoid those possible clarifications or changes. The solution to this dilemma lies in full disclosure of the problem to the client and in following the client's informed wishes.

Similarly, if clients are really going to give informed consent or make informed decisions, legal negotiators should tell clients all their options. In the above example, for instance, a legal negotiator should discuss the possibility of making a counter-offer— along with the negotiator's view about how the other side might react to it and the risks of not accepting the pending offer. It is often difficult to explain the options in a way that leaves the client with any real choice—particularly when the legal negotiator has formulated an opinion as to what ought to be done.

The ego involvement of lawyers—the lawyer's level of risk taking, anger with the opposing negotiator, or personal financial or social considerations—is a particular problem in the context of obtaining informed consent. Robert Bastress and Joseph Harbaugh in their book, *Interviewing, Counseling, and Negotiating: Skills for Effective Representation*, accurately point out that lawyers may consciously or unconsciously manipulate the client's expectations to assure the client's consent to the bargaining outcome that the lawyer obtains or to meet the lawyer's needs rather than the client's. For example, Bastress and Harbaugh point out that lawyers with an above-average fear of failure may manipulate a client's expectations by offering information that the expected settlement will be less than the lawyer actually anticipates; likewise, those with high risk-taking ego can overly raise expectations to support a more aggressive approach. Friendly or hostile relations with the opposing negotiator may also subtly influence the lawyer's evaluation of an offer.

Lawyers must be constantly on guard against letting their ego involvement distort informed client decision making. Bastress and Harbaugh suggest six steps to check the influence of your ego involvement and to gauge negotiating success in addition to apparent client satisfaction:

(1) use "client-centered" counseling to (a) isolate the client's goals and the client's needs and (b) communicate your candid appraisal of potential outcomes;

(2) involve the client in understanding and selecting the bargaining options, strategy, and tactics;

(3) assess constantly (a) your personal involvement and feelings about the case and the opposing negotia-

tor and (b) the influence of those factors on your client counseling or negotiation;

(4) plan carefully and in detail;

(5) reassess your ego involvement after the completion of the negotiation; and

(6) modify your preparation and execution of future negotiations based on that critical self-assessment.

In sum, legal negotiators may not be very comfortable with making trial outcome predictions to clients or with presenting the options fairly when they have strong personal feelings (coupled with a financial interest) about the advisability of rejecting or accepting a settlement offer. In the long run, however, fully informed clients will likely be more satisfied with decisions they really have made themselves. The clients who will be the least likely to be satisfied will be those who have been "kept in the dark" about the developments in their deals or lawsuits and who have been consistently told what to do by lawyers who thought they knew what was best for their clients.

Realistically, legal negotiators lack effective ways of evaluating the importance of intangible factors that play an important role in real client decision making and client satisfaction. For example, clients, not their lawyers, know best how to put a dollar value on avoiding the stress of trial or further harm to an already strained continuing relationship. Clients also know better how much risk they are willing to tolerate or how important it is to them to have their day in court to expose publicly the defendant's outrageous conduct. A lawyer's obligation is to help clients fully understand the choices, not to choose for them or to let the lawyer's personal ego involvement distort informed decision making.

Clashes between clients and their lawyers over moral issues, approaches, and views of fairness and justice ultimately are handled by withdrawal. Rule 1.16(b)(4) of the ABA's *Model Rules* allows a lawyer to withdraw when "a client insists upon taking action that the lawyer considers repugnant or with which the lawyer has a fundamental disagreement." Disciplinary Rule 2-110 in the ABA's *Model Code* allows a lawyer to withdraw if the client "[i]nsists, in a matter not pending before a tribunal, that the lawyer engage in conduct that is contrary to the judgment and advice of the lawyer but not prohibited under the Disciplinary Rules."

4. THE LAWYER AS THE CLIENT'S AGENT

Another important consequence of a lawyer representing a client in a legal negotiation relates to the role of the lawyer as the client's agent. In general, a lawyer has no implied power to compromise and settle a client's claim or cause of action merely by virtue of being retained by the client. Thus, the client may ignore a settlement made by the lawyer without specific authorization or conferral of authority. The client may proceed with the lawsuit, institute a new lawsuit, or request the court set aside the settlement and reinstate the action.

An exception to this general rule arises when (1) no opportunity for consultation with the client exists and (2) prompt action is necessary to protect the client's interest which the lawyer was retained to represent. In absence of an emergency, however, specific authority (or subsequent ratification by the client) is required before a compromise or settlement by the lawyer will be binding on the client.

When a client has expressly conferred authority, a lawyer may settle any matter in the action. Under those circumstances, the client is bound—even though the lawyer negligently recommended the settlement— because of the rule that the acts or omissions of an agent acting within the scope of authority are regarded as the acts of the person whom the agent represents. In other words, the lawyer's professional negligence is imputed to the client, who is bound thereby. The client's only recourse is an action against the lawyer for malpractice in causing the settlement to be accepted.

D. BASIC TYPES OF LEGAL NEGOTIATIONS

Negotiation by lawyers in a legal context can be divided into six basic categories:

(1) contractual transactions;

(2) civil disputes;

(3) labor-management negotiations;

(4) criminal cases;

(5) divorce and domestic relations problems; and

(6) international legal negotiations.

Each category reflects to some degree a specialized kind of negotiation. Competent lawyers adjust their approach to reflect the customs, practices, and peculiarities of purpose prevailing in each category.

1. CONTRACTUAL TRANSACTIONS

One category of legal negotiations lawyers conduct relates to transactions between parties. This type of negotiation arises in a wide array of settings— including sales of goods, securities, real property, services, and operating businesses. From a legal perspective, the hallmark of this kind of negotiation is a voluntary exchange on the part of the parties. Written contracts often, but not always, memorialize the exchange. These agreements regulating the transactions are essentially legislative in nature: they are directed primarily at the future conduct of the parties and the parties' respective rights.

Four aspects of this type of negotiation should be kept in mind. First, most transactions are consensual. In this type of negotiation, either party can "walk away" from the deal or decide to do business with someone else. Market conditions generally dictate the degree of freedom that the parties have. However, most transactions have to be mutually beneficial to the parties for a deal to be made.

Second, a thorough knowledge of the business facts associated with a particular type of transaction will dramatically enhance a legal negotiator's effectiveness in this type of negotiation. In unfamiliar business contexts, legal negotiators should educate themselves about the nature of the transaction, its purpose, the benefits each side seeks to obtain, the "selling" points, and the industry. General information can usually be obtained from specialized legal and nonlegal publications, continuing legal education materials, and other lawyers. The best source for particularized information is usually the client.

Third, transactions may reflect a continuing relationship or a short-term exchange. In transactions requiring cooperation between the parties over a long period, parties normally will be concerned with promoting harmonious relations from the outset.

Fourth, excessive aggressiveness, intimidation, or unreasonableness in negotiating transactions may "kill the deal"—unless a monopolistic situation or one in which extreme inequality of bargaining power exists. Thus, by insisting on "excessive" safeguards compared to the standard industry custom and practice, legal negotiators may cause their clients (and themselves) to be seen as rude, stubborn "nitpickers." This adversarial approach is likely to be seen as a breach of etiquette and will generate unnecessary distrust and hostility.

An important element of a legal negotiator's preparation should include acquiring knowledge of traditional industry standards, customs, and practices. One way is to examine successful agreements made by others in the industry to see how the various legal problems have been handled. Another way is to consult specialized legal materials if they are available.

2. CIVIL DISPUTES

Another important category of legal negotiations arises in the context of civil disputes. In these situations, one or both of the parties are asserting legal rights and remedies enforceable in court. Such disputes usually center on one or more of issues. First, in light of the facts of the particular dispute, does the applicable substantive law provide any right to recover? Second, is the complaining party entitled to the kind of remedy sought, such as an injunction or a constructive trust? Third, is the size of recovery sought justified by the provable facts and likely trial outcome?

The most significant aspect of negotiation of civil disputes is that if the parties do not reach a voluntary settlement themselves, a final resolution of the dispute will be made by a court or some other authorized decision maker, such as an arbitrator. Thus, if a party fails to defend the lawsuit or loses on the merits, that party can be compelled through a judgment or order to honor the legal rights of the opposing party. This type of negotiation is essentially adjudicatory in which the parties are concerned how the given rules will be applied to particular facts. Under these circumstances, much higher levels of aggressiveness and unreasonableness can occur than would be tolerated in the negotiation of consensual transactions.

Another important aspect of negotiation of civil disputes is the role of insurance coverage. Today, insurance is available for most forms of liability-creating activities—ranging from products liability and malpractice insurance to compulsory automobile coverage. The existence of insurance introduces issues of coverage, claim adjustors, and insurance defense counsel into the settlement and trial process—and, with them, institutional biases and concerns with which the plaintiff must deal. What are the policy limits? Is this claim going to encourage others to make similar claims—in other words, will it "open the flood gates"? Is payment of this claim going to harm the insurer's reputation?

Like transactions, civil disputes can involve single occurrences in which the parties to the dispute are not likely to have future contact (such as automobile accidents). Similarly, civil disputes can also involve problems in a long-term or continuing relationship (such as franchises or other distribution arrangements). Yet even when the parties will never have future contact, their legal negotiators may have to deal with each other again or with others who hear of their conduct in the dispute.

3. LABOR-MANAGEMENT NEGOTIATIONS

The primary purpose of a labor union is to protect its members by seeking fair remuneration and favorable working conditions. Federal law extensively regulates labor relations in the United States. Title 29 of the *United States Code* imposes a duty on employers and the employees' representatives to bargain collectively. Labor and management are required to meet at reasonable times and confer in good faith concerning wages, hours, and other terms and conditions of employment. This duty, however, does not compel either side to agree to a proposal nor does it require concession making. Failure to agree, however, raises the possibility of labor using its power to strike or management using its power to close, relocate, or lockout. Thus, the pressure to settle is often high.

Labor-management negotiations have characteristics of both transactions and civil disputes. They resemble transactions because the negotiations take place in the context of continuing relationships and are directed toward contractual agreements. Like transactions, often no wrong exists for which a judicially cognizable remedy is available—at least not without exhausting the administrative procedures mandated by the labor laws. Furthermore, the function of collective bargaining is essentially legislative: the parties are establishing rules that will govern their relations in the future. There is also an emphasis on seeking ways to maximize the benefits of the agreement to both management and labor (as opposed to the "win-loss" approach of most litigation).

On the other hand, labor-management negotiations resemble civil disputes because the parties have a legal duty to bargain. Like civil disputes, the labor-management negotiations often reflect a high degree of adversariness. They also are noted for tough bargaining and "psychological warfare."

Frequently, lawyers will be the bargainers for management while non-lawyers will be the bargainers for labor. Constituency pressure is very significant in collective bargaining. For example, the union negotiator will often be very sensitive to the reaction of the bargaining committee and represented rank-and-file employees to the negotiations. The parties usually bargain within a specific time-frame (generally sixty or ninety days). The presence of a deadline is usually a significant factor influencing the negotiation. Furthermore, in this type of negotiation, the negotiators are often highly concerned about the effect of the current collective bargaining agreement on future ones.

Collective bargaining usually involves multiple issues. Intentional ambiguity in particular clauses of the agreement is sometimes used to resolve difficult issues. This approach is possible because collective bargaining agreements provide methods of resolving disputes that arise during the term of the agreement, such as arbitration. Another characteristic of labor-management agreements is that they can be, and sometimes are, modified mid-term through mutual agreement or past practice.

4. CRIMINAL CASES

Criminal law declares what conduct in a jurisdiction is illegal and prescribes the punishment to be imposed for such conduct. The law is primarily directed at protecting society from criminal misconduct, but it concurrently protects defendants from overzealous or unjustified prosecution and punishment. The Sixth Amendment to the U.S. Constitution guarantees defendants in criminal cases the right to assistance of counsel—private counsel, public defenders, or appointed lawyers. Thus, on one side are defendants and their lawyers; on the other side are prosecuting attorneys who represent the interests of the government and society.

About the same percentage of criminal cases "settle" as civil cases. One reason for this high settlement rate is that the government is usually in a position of strength—and thus defendants have little to gain by going to trial. Another reason is a practical one—if a large number of cases did not settle, the courts would be bogged down in providing criminal defendants trials.

In a criminal context, lawyers attempt to settle in several ways. First, defense attorneys may try to convince prosecutors not to charge potential defendants at all. Second, they may seek to convince prosecutors to recommend an adjournment in contemplation of dismissal (in which the charges will be dismissed if the person is not arrested again during a certain future period) or to use some other similar procedure that is available locally. Third, they may seek immunity from prosecution for potential defendants in return for testimony in other criminal cases. Fourth, they may engage in plea bargaining. This form of settlement often involves a guilty plea to a lesser offense or to only one or some counts of a multicount indictment by a defendant in return for a lighter sentence than that possible for the graver charge. The bargaining may also concern the evidence to be admitted and the recommendation of parole.

Plea bargaining procedures in the federal courts are regulated by Rule 11(c) of the Federal Rules of Criminal Procedure. Rule 11(c) covers, *inter alia*, the following: plea bargaining procedure; required disclosure of the plea agreement; judicial consideration of the plea; court acceptance or rejection; inadmissibility of plea discussions and pleas; and required records of plea proceedings. This rule, however, does not address the underlying practical and philosophical aspects of plea bargaining.

Like the involvement of insurance companies in civil disputes, institutional factors affect the settlement of criminal cases. Prosecutors, public defenders, and local criminal attorneys must deal with each other on a continuing basis. Thus, their conduct in one case may affect another. Both public defenders and prosecutors are concerned about case load and administrative efficiency. Prosecutors are concerned about maintaining good relations with the police and the public. Likewise, raises and promotions of prosecutors as well as their reelection may be affected by their "win-loss" record.

There is one key aspect of negotiating in a criminal context that defense attorneys should recognize from the outset: interpersonal factors affect the exercise of the prosecutor's discretion. Thus, in the routine case, a defense attorney should strive to get the prosecutor to know and like the defendant. From the prosecutor's perspective, perhaps the most important task is making guilty defendants and their lawyers think that they are getting a good deal.

5. DIVORCE AND DOMESTIC RELATIONS

Another distinct type of legal negotiation involves divorce and domestic relations problems. Like transactions and collective bargaining agreements, this type of negotiation is essentially legislative in nature:

it is designed to govern the future status, rights, and obligations of the parties. In divorce and domestic relations negotiations, the parties often have high emotional and psychological involvement in the dispute. For example, the parties may be spiteful or bitter and resist rational solutions. The rights and interests of third parties, such as the children of the parties, may be important factors. A high degree of pressure to reach a settlement usually exists.

6. INTERNATIONAL LEGAL NEGOTIATIONS

Another important category of legal negotiations conducted by lawyers arises in the context of international transactions and disputes. Three distinguishing characteristics associated with this type of legal negotiation should be taken into account. First, negotiation in an international legal context often involves cultural barriers that may make it more difficult to reach an agreement. Second, it often is complicated by language barriers, which increases the chances of misunderstanding; these barriers are often compounded by the use of translators. Third, it is often influenced by political considerations.

E. SCOPE OF THE DISCUSSION

Most of the discussion in this text is directed (unless otherwise stated) toward negotiating civil disputes. This type of negotiation permits a broad range of permissible behavior. However, it does not raise (1) the complicated issues of fairness, ethics, and

public policy involved in criminal and domestic
relations cases; (2) the group dynamics issues raised
by labor negotiations; nor (3) the cross-cultural and
political problems arising in an international context.
Nonetheless, much of what is stated about negotiating civil disputes applies to criminal cases, labor-
management negotiations, divorce negotiations, and
international legal negotiations.

F. LEGAL FACTORS THAT SHOULD BE
CONSIDERED PRIOR TO ENTERING
INTO NEGOTIATIONS

Prior to entering into legal negotiations, several
legal factors should be considered. First, will settlement offers and discussions be admissible at trial?
Second, do procedural rules (such as Rule 68 of the
Federal Rules of Civil Procedure) impact offers of
compromise? Third, what is the effect of negotiations
on the statute of limitations? It is obviously important to know the answers prior to entering into
negotiations.

1. SETTLEMENT OFFERS AND DISCUSSIONS
AS EVIDENCE AT TRIAL

Under the common law, evidence of offers to
compromise a dispute is inadmissible at trial for the
purpose of proving the offeror's liability. There are
three possible theoretical bases for this rule. One is
the "English" or "contract" theory, in which offers are
assumed to be made without prejudice; unless the

offer is accepted and a contract actually formed, the offer has no evidentiary force. A second basis for this rule is the "relevancy" theory, in which the offer to compromise is viewed as demonstrating a desire for peace and not as admitting any wrong done. Thus, evidence of the offer is irrelevant to actual liability and is excluded. A third basis for this rule is the "privileged exception" theory, which is based on the policy of the courts to encourage settlements.

None of these theories, however, generally excludes from evidence admitted statements of fact, collateral statements, or conduct not forming the actual compromise offer. If the rules of evidence allow such statements or conduct to be used at trial against the party making them, the openness of communication during actual negotiations may be substantially lessened. Nonetheless, in some jurisdictions, a statement made in the course of negotiations or in a settlement offer may constitute an admission of an independent fact pertinent to an issue between the parties.

In those jurisdictions allowing the admission of statements of fact, collateral statements, and conduct occurring in conjunction with settlement discussions or offers, the critical question is whether the statement is inseparable from the offer of compromise or so closely connected with it to be excludable from evidence. For example, if liability were conceded and negotiations were held merely to establish the amount or worth of the damage or loss, the offer of compromise would be admissible to establish liability though not as proof of the amount of the loss.

The phrasing of the statement or admission is also important. A concession that is hypothetical or conditional cannot be interpreted as an assertion representing the party's actual belief. For example, the statement, "Let's assume, just for the purposes of these negotiations, that my client was negligent, what would you think the damages ought to be?" is conditional and inadmissible. On the other hand, an unconditional assertion is admissible notwithstanding the motive that may have prompted it. For example, the statement, "Okay, my client was negligent, let's talk about damages" is unconditional and admissible.

Because of the risk of admissibility of statements made during the course of negotiations in those jurisdictions following the common law, lawyers have developed various methods to deal with admissibility problems. One solution has been to refuse to negotiate until the other side agrees in writing that anything said is "without prejudice" to the client's rights. Absent such agreements, lawyers have avoided making admissions in settlement negotiations by phrasing all factual statements hypothetically and by including disclaimers in all writings so that the statements will be of no value as evidence: for example, "Our client admits, for the sake of these negotiations only, ..." An even safer method has been to preface the entire statement, letter, or discussion with the following type of statement: "This claim is doubtful and disputed, and one upon which liability, damage, and all other contentions of fact are expressly denied. Anything I state automatically includes this disclaimer."

Rule 408 of the Federal Rules of Evidence removes many of the problems about statements and offers made in settlement discussions. Rule 408 specifically excludes evidence of furnishing or offering "a valuable consideration in compromising or attempting to compromise a claim which was disputed as to either validity or amount." This rule is based on the public policy favoring compromise. Thus, like the common law, Rule 408 makes explicit offers of compromise inadmissible, but it uses a privilege theory to alter the common-law rule by extending inadmissibility to "conduct or statements made in compromise negotiations."

The "valuable consideration" language in Rule 408 is intended to do away with the so-called "nuisance offers"—ones of only minimal value in relation to the size of the injury. This addition, however, has been criticized as contributing unnecessary ambiguity to the rule; it is not yet clear how valuable the consideration must be.

Rule 408 also departs from the common law by including disputes as to either "validity or amount." Under Rule 408, the compromise offer is inadmissible to prove either liability or the amount of liability. Rule 408 also contains two limitations on the general exclusionary treatment for evidence of offers or agreements of compromise. First, Rule 408 does not require the exclusion of any evidence that is otherwise discoverable merely because it is presented in the course of compromise negotiations. This exception was added to make sure that litigants could not avoid the admission of relevant and discoverable facts by admitting them in compromise negotiations. In other words, admissions in compromise negotiations are admissible if they are also discoverable through proper independent means.

Second, evidence of compromise and offers to compromise may be used to prove (1) a consequential, material fact in issue other than validity or invalidity of the claim or its amount or (2) to prove bias or prejudice of a witness. This provision allows a "collateral use" of the evidence for a purpose other than proving liability; it arises most often in multiple party cases for the purpose of impeaching the credibility of a person not a party to the compromise agreement. A question still exists whether courts should allow statements made during compromise negotiations to be used to impeach the parties to the compromise. Such use would seem to violate the policy upon which the rule is based. Neither the common law nor Rule 408 applies until there is an attempt to compromise a disputed claim.

Many states have now passed rules of evidence the same as or similar to Rule 408. Other states have attempted to codify the common-law rules. The wise lawyer will become familiar with the rules in the relevant jurisdiction. It is otherwise a trap for the unwary or unsophisticated lawyer who might not be careful enough in the choice of terms or phrasing of factual statements in the context of settlement negotiations.

Rules 409 and 410 of the Federal Rules of Evidence also have a bearing on settlement agreements. Rule 409 provides that "[e]vidence of furnishing or offering or promising to pay medical, hospital, or similar expenses occasioned by an injury is not admissible to prove liability for the injury." Rule 409 is based not only on the policy encouraging settlement but also on the policy of encouraging the prompt assistance of injured persons by the defendant or the insurance company. This rule, however, does not cover conduct or statements that are not an integral part of this payment. Rule 409 is consistent with the common-law rule in most states that evidence of medical assistance is inadmissible to establish liability of the party rendering such assistance.

Rule 410 deals specifically with the use of evidence gained from plea bargaining in criminal cases. This rule is much stricter than Rule 408 and specifically excludes plea negotiation evidence from impeachment proceedings.

2. PROCEDURAL RULES AFFECTING OFFERS OF COMPROMISE

Rule 68 of the Federal Rules of Civil Procedure and similar state statutes and rules provide procedural incentives to settle. These rules have not been used frequently in the past, but there is presently a trend toward their greater use and a greater awareness of their potential impact. Under Federal Rule 68, for example, prior to 10 days before the trial begins, a party defending against a claim may serve upon the adverse party an offer to allow judgment to be taken against the defending party for the money or property or to the effect specified in the offer, with costs then accrued. If that offer is not accepted within 10 days by filing written notice, the unaccepted offer is deemed withdrawn and evidence thereof is not admissible except in a proceeding to determine costs. If the judgment finally obtained by the offeree is not more favorable than the offer, the offeree must pay the costs incurred after the making of the offer. The fact that an offer is made but not accepted, however, does not preclude a subsequent offer.

Furthermore, under Federal Rule 68, when the liability of one party to another has been determined by verdict or order or judgment, but the amount or extent of the liability remains to be determined by further proceedings, the party adjudged liable may make an offer of judgment. Such an offer of judgment has the same effect as an offer made before trial if it is served within a reasonable time not less than 10 days prior to the commencement of hearings to determine the amount or extent of liability.

The most important issue surrounding Rule 68 is whether the costs to be paid by the losing party will include attorney's fees, which usually make up the greatest part of the cost of litigation. Contrary to English practice, attorney's fees in the United States have not generally been assessed against losing parties unless there is express statutory authorization for them. Exceptions have been made to the "American rule," however, and there is a strong policy argument in favor of including the attorney's fees in the "costs incurred" provision of Rule 68. Some courts are presently awarding attorney's fees as a means of promoting the policy of the rule, though usually still in special circumstances. One study has recommended that Rule 68 be expressly amended to include the recovery of "costs and attorney's fees incurred."

3. EFFECT OF NEGOTIATIONS ON THE STATUTE OF LIMITATIONS

One of the choices that plaintiffs must make is whether to file suit before commencing settlement negotiations. Particularly in business settings, there is great reluctance to sue a fellow merchant. There is, however, a danger that negotiations may continue until the statute of limitations has run, thereby providing the other party with a defense against suit.

Absent a showing of wrongful conduct by the potential defendant, courts uniformly hold that the mere fact that settlement negotiations are underway does not of itself prevent the statute of limitations from running. This result may occur even when it seems clear that the defendant in fact intended to settle but did not. Furthermore, even when the defendant's actions would create justifiable reliance at one point in time, the defendant may be allowed to plead statute of limitations as a defense if the defendant's conduct was broken off—leaving the plaintiff sufficient time to file a complaint.

G. SELF-TESTS

Before reading subsequent chapters, it will be useful if you complete the following four "self-tests."

Feedback on these tests will be given at appropriate points in the discussion ahead.

1. SELF-TEST 1

Everyone brings a set of ideas, attitudes, and probable approaches to legal negotiations. These elements were formed from prior legal negotiating experiences, if any, from the many nonlegal negotiating experiences in life, and from one's general approach to life. In legal negotiations, lawyers engage in identifiable patterns of behavior, approaches, and attitudes. Recognizing and understanding these patterns are an important part of becoming a more effective legal negotiator.

The following self-test helps you consider what lawyers perceive as characteristics of effective legal negotiators. For purposes of this self-test, assume that you are going to attempt to settle a pending civil lawsuit through negotiation and that you want to be as effective a legal negotiator as possible. Which of the following characteristics would you want to display in that negotiation? Would you want to be viewed as: (check if you would)

1.	_X_	Headstrong	8.	___	Convincing
2.	___	Gentle	9.	_X_	Trustful
3.	___	Obliging	10.	___	Bluffer
4.	_X_	Prepared	11.	___	Loud
5.	_X_	Perceptive	12.	_X_	Analytical
6.	___	Forgiving	13.	_X_	Honest
7.	_X_	Self-Controlled	14.	___	Greedy

15. ____ Irritating	27. ____ Impatient
16. ____ Legally Astute	28. ____ Staller
17. ____ Obstinate	29. ____ Complaining
18. ____ Effective Trial	30. _x_ Ethical
Lawyer	31. ____ Conniving
19. _x_ Adaptable	32. ____ Quarrelsome
20. ____ Dignified	33. _x_ Realistic
21. ____ Intolerant	34. _x_ Versatile
22. _x_ Reasonable	35. _x_ Creative
23. _x_ Patient	36. ____ Experienced
24. _x_ Rational	37. ____ Skillful at Reading
25. _x_ Trustworthy	Your Opponent's Cues
26. ____ Tactless	38. ____ Emotional

2. SELF-TEST 2

Assume again that you are going to attempt to settle a civil lawsuit. In the following self-test, choose between the following pairs of descriptions or approaches. Based on your present ideas, attitudes, and approaches to negotiation, which one of the two descriptions or approaches would you tend more toward? Would you tend to: (check (a) or (b) but not both)

1. ____ (a) be cooperative *or*
   ____ (b) be competitive.
2. ____ (a) be obstructive *or*
   ____ (b) be forthright.
3. ____ (a) be courteous *or*
   ____ (b) be attacking.

4. ____ (a) be fair *or*
   ____ (b) be ambitious.
5. ____ (a) be personable *or*
   ____ (b) be forceful.
6. ____ (a) be clever *or*
   ____ (b) be sincere.
7. ____ (a) not be willing to "stretch the facts" *or*
   ____ (b) be willing to "stretch the facts."
8. ____ (a) be aggressive *or*
   ____ (b) be friendly.
9. ____ (a) be tough *or*
   ____ (b) be fair-minded.
10. ____ (a) take a realistic opening position *or*
    ____ (b) make high opening demands.
11. ____ (a) be facilitating *or*
    ____ (b) be rigid.
12. ____ (a) use threats *or*
    ____ (b) avoid threats.
13. ____ (a) be interested in a "fair" settlement for all
             parties concerned *or*
    ____ (b) be especially interested in obtaining a
             profitable fee for yourself.
14. ____ (a) stick to your position *or*
    ____ (b) be willing to move from your position.
15. ____ (a) be interested in personally outmaneuvering
             opposing counsel *or*
    ____ (b) not be especially concerned about outdoing
             opposing counsel.
16. ____ (a) not use a take-it-or-leave-it approach *or*
    ____ (b) use a take-it-or-leave-it approach.
17. ____ (a) be sociable *or*
    ____ (b) be dominating.

18. ____ (a) be tactful *or*
____ (b) be egotistical.

Now calculate a "reference number" for this self-test using the form below. If you checked the particular item listed, put a "1" in the space provided below (*e.g.*, put a "1" in the blank if you checked item 1(a), 2(b), 3(a), 4(a), etc.) and then calculate a total, which will be a number between 1 and 18.

1. (a) ____   10. (a) ____
2. (b) ____   11. (a) ____
3. (a) ____   12. (b) ____
4. (a) ____   13. (a) ____
5. (a) ____   14. (b) ____
6. (b) ____   15. (b) ____
7. (a) ____   16. (a) ____
8. (b) ____   17. (a) ____
9. (b) ____   18. (a) ____

Total _____ ("Reference Number")

3. SELF-TEST 3

Assume again that you are going to attempt to settle a civil lawsuit. In the following self-test, choose between the pairs of descriptions or approaches. Which one of the two descriptions or approaches would you tend to prefer—based on your present ideas, attitudes, and probable approaches to legal negotiation? (Check (a) or (b) but not both.)

1. In terms of basic bargaining approach, would you

____ (a) establish a bargaining position and then narrow the differences through argument and compromise *or*

____ (b) focus on satisfying the preferences or needs of the parties?

2. In terms of bargaining issues, would you

____ (a) formulate them as resources that must be divided *or*

____ (b) problems that must be solved?

3. In terms of the bargaining "resources," would you

____ (a) focus on how to divide the limited resources *or*

____ (b) work to create additional resources?

4. In terms of how intangible items (such as pain and suffering) are treated in a negotiation, would you

____ (a) convert such items into dollars and divide them through bargaining as any other dollar item *or*

____ (b) refuse to convert intangible items into fungible commodities to be divided through bargaining?

5. In terms of conceptualizing the negotiation process, would you tend to view it as a process with

____ (a) winners and losers *or*

____ (b) a possibly mutually beneficial outcome?

6. In terms of your approach to a negotiation involving a breach of contract, would you tend to

_____ (a) view the negotiation solely in terms of legal entitlements (*i.e.*, legal rights and remedies enforceable in court) *or*

_____ (b) use legal entitlements as one of several factors in determining a solution?

7. In terms of an overall strategy, would you

_____ (a) prefer to take an "adversarial" approach *or*

_____ (b) prefer to engage in mutual "problem solving"?

4. SELF-TEST 4

To gain perspective on the possible problems relating to legal negotiation, indicate how you would handle the following situations.

Situation 1. Assume that an insurance company is defending a lawsuit brought by a passenger allegedly injured in an automobile accident with the insured. Assume that you represent the plaintiff. The plaintiff has told you that the plaintiff would be quite willing to settle the lawsuit for $50,000. In the course of negotiations with the insurance company's lawyer, assume that you are directly asked whether the plaintiff would be willing to accept $50,000 in settlement. As a negotiating tactic, would you deny that your client would be willing to settle the lawsuit for that amount?

_____ (a) Yes *or*
_____ (b) No.

Situation 2. Assume the same facts as described in *Situation 1*, except that the plaintiff has given you specific instructions to accept an offer of $50,000. As a negotiating tactic, would you deny that you had the authority to compromise the case for that amount?

_____ (a) Yes *or*
_____ (b) No.

Situation 3. Assume the same facts as described in *Situation 1*, except that the insurance company offers $60,000 in settlement and you have told the insurance company's lawyer that you "believe that we have an agreement." As a negotiating tactic, would you then have your client reject the agreement and raise your demands?

_____ (a) Yes *or*
_____ (b) No.

Situation 4. Assume the same facts as described in *Situation 1*, except that you have just discovered a recent judicial decision that would limit the plaintiff's recoverable damages to $15,000. Would you disclose it and settle for $15,000? If the insurance company has offered $60,000 to settle the case, would you quickly accept the offer before the insurance company's counsel learns of the new judicial decision?

_____ (a) Yes *or*
_____ (b) No.

Situation 5. Assume the same facts as described in *Situation 1*, except that you have just learned that your client had been drinking martinis for three hours at an office party shortly before the accident. Assume that under the law of the controlling jurisdiction, it is certain that the plaintiff would be found to have been contributorily negligent (completely barring the plaintiff's recovery). If you were asked in a negotiation whether the plaintiff had been drinking prior to the accident, would you deny that the plaintiff had been drinking?

_____ (a) Yes *or*

_____ (b) No *or*

_____ (c) Say that you didn't know for sure and then talk to the client.

Would you drop the lawsuit voluntarily or would you try to quickly settle the case before the insurance company learns of these adverse facts?

_____ (d) Voluntarily drop the lawsuit *or*

_____ (e) Try to quickly settle the case.

Situation 6. Assume the same facts described in *Situation 1*, except that now you represent the insurance company in the above dispute. Would you be willing to feign an internal dispute between another lawyer and yourself to trick the plaintiff's lawyer into thinking that you really want to help the plaintiff?

_____ (a) Yes *or*

_____ (b) No.

Situation 7. Again, assume that you represent the insurance company in *Situation 1*. Would you state that "the facts appear to relieve the insurer of liability" when new adverse factual information (not yet known to the other side) clearly shows the facts to be to the contrary?

_____ (a) Yes *or*

_____ (b) No.

Situation 8. Assume that you represent the husband in a divorce action. Assume that you are developing your opening position. As a negotiating tactic, would you demand custody of the children even though your client has specifically told you that he does not want custody?

_____ (a) Yes *or*

_____ (b) No.

Situation 9. Assume that the police have finally caught a rapist and you are the prosecutor. After the rapist was charged, you entered into plea bargain negotiations. While those negotiations are going on, you discover that the police clearly violated the constitutional rights of the defendant. Without the evidence that would be excluded, you have no case. Do you accept the plea bargain or do you disclose the violation and let the rapist go free?

_____ (a) Accept the plea bargain *or*

_____ (b) Disclose the violation and let the rapist go free.

Situation 10. Assume that you represent management in a labor negotiation. Your client wants you to refuse to negotiate seriously with the union because the company is overstocked and management thinks that a strike will break the union. Would you follow your client's instructions?

_____ (a) Yes *or*

_____ (b) No.

Situation 11. Assume that you represent the plaintiff in an action to collect a debt. Your client, in a passing fit of anger, has told you that "if the defendant does not agree to pay half the debt in settlement, the defendant is likely to be fit with a concrete collar for use at the bottom of the river." As a negotiating tactic, would you mention your client's statement?

_____ (a) Yes *or*

_____ (b) No.

Situation 12. Assume the same facts as described in *Situation 11*, except that the threat is not an idle one. As a negotiating tactic, would you mention it if it were really true?

_____ (a) Yes *or*

_____ (b) No.

Situation 13. Assume that you represent the plaintiff in a contract dispute. Would you threaten to file a civil action for damages to break a deadlock in the negotiations?

_____ (a) Yes *or*

_____ (b) No.

Situation 14. Assume that you represent the wife in a divorce action. Your client discloses information that leads you to believe that the husband has committed acts constituting child abuse. The husband refuses to negotiate in any reasonable manner. Would you threaten to report the husband for past child abuse to induce serious settlement discussions?

_____ (a) Yes *or*

_____ (b) No.

Situation 15. Assume the same facts as *Situation 14*, except that the husband is in a politically sensitive position in which adverse news coverage would be extremely harmful. Would you threaten to publicize his past child abuse to gain better settlement terms?

_____ (a) Yes *or*

_____ (b) No.

Situation 16. Assume that you are negotiating with a lawyer whom you realize is inexperienced and poorly prepared. In the negotiation, the opposing lawyer makes many unnecessary and unwise concessions. In other words, the opposing lawyer is an incompetent negotiator. Would you "sit back," do nothing, and allow that lawyer to "give the case away" or would you help that lawyer realize what needs to be done to competently represent the other side?

_____ (a) I would "sit back," do nothing, and allow the lawyer to "give the case away" *or*

_____ (b) I would help that lawyer realize what needs to be done to competently represent the other side.

Situation 17. Assume that you face the same scenario as described in *Situation 16*, except that the other side's negotiating incompetence is the result of the lawyer's personal drinking problem. Assuming that you could take advantage of this situation to negotiate an unfair settlement, would you settle only at an objectively fair amount?

_____ (a) Yes *or*

_____ (b) No.

Situation 18. Assume that you represent the husband in a divorce action and you are negotiating with the wife's lawyer. Assume that your client wants custody of his three-year-old daughter and that his wife is willing to give up custody in return for a very substantial alimony payment. Assume that you would be able to minimize highly adverse information about your client (that would possibly influence the court to refuse to award custody to the husband based on possible harm to the child) at the time the settlement is presented to the court. Would you make the alimony offer that your client wants you to make?

_____ (a) Yes *or*

_____ (b) No.

Would you seek custody of the child for the husband in the first place?

_____ (c) Yes *or*

_____ (d) No.

Would you refrain from using your advocacy skills to the fullest and disclose the possible harm at the time the settlement agreement is presented to the court for approval?

_____ (e) Yes *or*

_____ (f) No.

Situation 19. Assume that you are negotiating on behalf of your client to buy a piece of real estate. Assume you are authorized to offer $1,000,000 for the property and would be most pleased to get the property for that amount (a fair market price). Before making an offer, however, you realize that because of recent developments, the out-of-state owner does not realize the current market value of the property has doubled. Assuming the owner would accept $500,000, would you offer that lower amount?

_____ (a) Yes *or*

_____ (b) No.

Would you disclose the recent developments?

_____ (c) Yes *or*

_____ (d) No.

Situation 20. Assume that you represent an insurance company and that you are defending a personal injury claim. Assume that the plaintiff's lawyer has seriously undervalued the case and has indicated that the plaintiff would be willing to settle for $50,000. Assume that it is probable that a trial verdict of at least five times that amount is likely. Would you settle the case for $50,000 (or less) when you know that this settlement is going to leave the

plaintiff bedridden and, because of continuing medical bills and expenses, destitute?

_____ (a) Yes *or*

_____ (b) No.

CHAPTER 2

"EFFECTIVE" AND "INEFFECTIVE" LEGAL NEGOTIATORS, LEGAL NEGOTIATING "STYLES" AND "STRATEGIES," AND THE "STAGES" OF LEGAL NEGOTIATIONS

An essential part of being an effective legal negotiator is the ability to recognize and understand the basic negotiating "styles" that legal negotiators typically adopt and the basic "strategies" that are possible in legal negotiation. In addition, it is essential to know the characteristics that make legal negotiators "effective" regardless of the style or strategy adopted. Furthermore, in light of this knowledge, it is critically important for legal negotiators to be able to consciously adopt a style and strategy appropriate to the situation. This chapter focuses primarily on basic strategic choices available in legal negotiations as well as basic elements and dynamics of legal negotiating styles.

A. CHARACTERISTICS OF "EFFECTIVE" LEGAL NEGOTIATORS

In the leading empirical study of legal negotiators conducted in 1976, Professor Gerald Williams, along with three colleagues, asked a large number of practicing lawyers to describe the characteristics of negotiators they regarded as "effective," "average," and "ineffective." Self-Test 1 in Chapter 1(G), above, reflects descriptions provided by those lawyers. Several of the descriptions are characteristics of legal negotiators who have been rated as effective negotiators. These characteristics are the ones that appear to underlie whatever negotiating style and strategy legal negotiators tend to follow and are ones that you should have checked in the self-test.

First, effective legal negotiators are seen as thoroughly *prepared* (#4).

Second, effective legal negotiators are seen as *legally astute* (#16). This characteristic means that they have done their homework by informing themselves about the legal and procedural ramifications of the case. It also means that they are able to make good judgments with respect to this information.

Third, effective legal negotiators are seen as *realistic* (#33), *rational* (#24), *analytical* (#12), and *reasonable* (#22). These traits mean more than "thinking like a lawyer." They impose limits on how far a negotiator may credibly go in stretching the interpretation of facts and making damage claims and other economic demands. These traits also limit the level of personal emotional involvement in the case.

Fourth, effective legal negotiators are seen as *creative* (#35), *versatile* (#34), and *adaptable* (#19). In other words, they are able to seek creative solutions and to compromise.

Fifth, effective legal negotiators are seen as *experienced* (#36). This characteristic is not surprising because most lawyers assume that negotiating effectiveness improves with experience. Professor Williams, however, suggests that the meaning of this characteristic is best illuminated by one lawyer's comment: "It is important to have enough experience in order that you have confidence in yourself and be able to convey that confidence."

Sixth, effective legal negotiators are seen as *ethical* (#30), *trustworthy* (#25), and *honest* (#13). As a general rule, they are also careful to observe the customs and courtesies of the bar.

Seventh, effective legal negotiators are seen as *self-controlled* (#7). They are not emotionally manipulated by others.

Eighth, effective legal negotiators are seen as *skillful at reading their opponents' cues* (#37). This trait refers not only to the ability to judge opponents' reactions in negotiating situations but also to learn affirmatively from their opponents.

Ninth, effective legal negotiators are seen as being *perceptive* (#5). This characteristic relates, in part, to the ability to perceive opponents' strategy and their subjective reaction to that strategy. It also relates to the ability to perceive the whole case accurately.

Tenth, effective legal negotiators are seen as *convincing* (#8).

Finally, effective legal negotiators are seen as *effective trial lawyers* (#18). One reason that effective legal negotiators are rated as effective trial lawyers may relate to other underlying shared characteristics, such as thoroughness of preparation, ability to perceive effects of tactics, and the ability to be convincing. Furthermore, if negotiators are considered weak trial lawyers, it will often prove more profitable to take them to trial rather than to agree to a reasonable settlement.

Because weak trial lawyers know that their clients would be poorly served by an inept trial of the case, weak lawyers discount the case as an inducement to the other side to settle and avoid the costs and benefits of trial. To be taken seriously, lawyers who negotiate legal disputes (as opposed to nonactionable matters) must either develop substantial expertise as trial lawyers, or must openly associate themselves with very effective trial counsel. This association might be accomplished through partnership, referral, or some other way.

B. CHARACTERISTICS OF "INEFFECTIVE" LEGAL NEGOTIATORS

In contrast to the characteristics of effective legal negotiators discussed in the preceding section, a flag of caution should be raised if you checked any of the following characteristics in Self-Test 1 in Chapter 1(G), above: *headstrong* (#1), *gentle* (#2), *obliging* (#3), *forgiving* (#6), *trustful* (#9), *bluffer* (#10), *loud* (#11), *greedy* (#14), *irritating* (#15), *obstinate* (#17), *dignified* (#20), *intolerant* (#21), *patient* (#23), *tactless* (#26), *impatient* (#27), *staller* (#28), *complaining* (#29), *conniving* (#31), *quarrelsome* (#32), and *emotional* (#38). These characteristics were found in Professor

Williams' study to be associated with ineffective legal negotiators.

C. LEGAL NEGOTIATING STYLES

1. "COOPERATIVE" VS. "COMPETITIVE" LEGAL NEGOTIATING STYLES

Professor Williams' research found that a high percentage of practicing lawyers follow one of two basic patterns of legal negotiation: (1) a "cooperative" style that moves *psychologically toward* the opposing negotiator or (2) a "competitive" style that moves *psychologically against* the opposing negotiator. If your total reference number for Self-Test 2 in Chapter 1(G), above, was nine, you are at the midpoint. If your total was ten or more, you generally tend more toward the cooperative style. If your total was less than nine, you tend more toward the competitive style. In addition, if your total reference number for Self-Test 2 is fourteen or more, you tend to be more cooperative than a large sample of second-year and third-year law students at the outset of law school negotiation classes. If your total was thirteen or less, you tend to be more competitive.

2. THE COOPERATIVE STYLE

In a scientifically selected sample of the practicing bar (but not with a sufficiently large percentage of women to provide reliable statistics on the distribution of women among the various categories), Professor Gerald Williams found that a cooperative approach was taken by 65% of the lawyers. A competitive approach was taken by 24% of the lawyers. These patterns were found to be so pervasive that only 11% failed to follow either of these approaches or any other identifiable pattern.

In this same sample, about half of the lawyers were rated as "effective" negotiators, 38% were rated as "average," and 12% were rated as "ineffective." Neither the cooperative nor the competitive pattern, however, had an exclusive claim on effectiveness. Of the lawyers who were rated as effective negotiators and who followed either a competitive or cooperative style, 6% used a competitive style while 38% used a cooperative style. The higher proportion of cooperative lawyers rated as effective, however, does suggest that it is more difficult to be an effective competitive negotiator than an effective cooperative one. With regard to average-rated negotiators who followed either a competitive or cooperative style, 10% used a competitive style while 24% used a cooperative style. For ineffective-rated negotiators, 8% used a competitive strategy while 2% used a cooperative style.

This subsection focuses on the basic elements and dynamics of the cooperative style—how this pattern of legal negotiation works and what specifically determines its effectiveness or ineffectiveness.

a. Basic Elements

The general approach adopted by effective cooperative negotiators is to negotiate in an objective, fair, and trustworthy way and to seek agreement by the open exchange of information. The basic dynamic of the cooperative style is *to move psychologically toward the opposing party.* Cooperatives communicate a sense of shared interests, values, and attitudes. They seek common ground and promote a trusting atmosphere. They use rational, logical persuasion as a means of seeking cooperation. They try to appear as not seeking a special advantage for self or client— they want to reach a fair outcome based on an objective analysis of the facts and the law.

Concessions play a critical role in the cooperative style. Concessions are one of the means of demonstrating the cooperative negotiator's own good faith. Cooperatives believe that this approach creates a moral obligation in the other side to reciprocate and induces like behavior. Thus, they make unilateral concessions to induce the other side to (1) reciprocate, (2) cooperate in openly and objectively resolving the problem, (3) forgo aggression, and (4) reach a solution.

Cooperative negotiators feel a high commitment to fairness and do not view negotiation as a game. To them, gamesmanship is ethically suspect. They feel that to move psychologically against another person to promote one's own self-interest is manipulative.

b. *Effective Cooperatives*

Professor Williams found that effective cooperative negotiators have six principal objectives or concerns. They have (1) a predominant concern with ethical conduct. They want to conduct themselves ethically.

They want (2) to maximize settlement for their clients, but this objective is tempered by (3) a basic concern for getting a fair settlement. In other words, these negotiators feel constrained in their conduct by a standard of fairness and ethical dealing. They are (4) concerned about their clients' needs and, if possible, (5) want to meet those needs without the necessity of litigation. They also want to (6) establish or maintain a good personal relationship with their opponents.

Effective cooperative negotiators are seen as *fair-minded*, *reasonable*, *objective*, *logical* (not emotional), and willing to move from their established positions. They take realistic opening positions (but leave room to negotiate), support their position with facts, and are forthright. They are seen as *wise*, *careful*, *organized*, and *cooperative*. They seek to facilitate agreement, avoid the use of threats, and accurately estimate the value of their cases; they are sensitive to the need of their clients and are willing to share information with their opponents.

Effective cooperative negotiators are *personable*. They are seen as *friendly*, *courteous*, *tactful*, and *sincere*. Nonetheless, they are not pushovers because, by definition, they are seen as effective.

c. Ineffective Cooperatives

Like effective cooperatives, ineffective cooperatives are seen as ethical, trustworthy, fair, personable, and experienced. Ineffective cooperatives, however, lack the skills and attitudes of their effective counterparts, such as being perceptive, convincing, or reasonable (realistic, rational, and analytical). Nor are they creative, self-controlled, versatile, objective, organized, or legally astute.

One mark of ineffective legal negotiators is the apparent inability to value cases and to convey their view of value convincingly. Research has shown that ineffective cooperative negotiators are perceived as being unsure of the value of the case (*conservative*, *staller*, *cautious*, *deliberate*). Likewise, ineffective competitive negotiators are seen as being unsure of the value of the case.

Professor Williams found that ineffective cooperatives are torn between being gentle, obliging, patient, moderate, and forgiving on one hand and being demanding and argumentative on the other. They tend to be somewhat idealistic, which may account for their lack of versatility, adaptability, creativity, and wisdom. Furthermore, they tend to be *trustful* of their opponents—they tend to believe what they are told.

d. Dangers of the Cooperative Style

The principal disadvantage of the cooperative style is its vulnerability to exploitation. It takes two persons to cooperate and to arrive at a maximum joint outcome (one that gives the greatest benefit and does the least harm to both sides). For the cooperative approach to be successful, both sides have to pursue that approach in good faith. In contrast, it only takes one person to engage in a strategic confrontation—to seek to intimidate and outmaneuver to maximize one side's gain.

When cooperative negotiators attempt to establish a cooperative, trusting atmosphere in a negotiation with a tough, non-cooperative opponent, cooperative lawyers have an alarming tendency to ignore the lack of reciprocal cooperation and to pursue their cooperative style unilaterally. Their basic style requires them to continue to discuss the case fairly and objectively, to make concessions about the weaknesses of their case, and to refrain from self-serving behavior.

In this situation, the tough negotiator is free to accept all of the fairness and cooperation without giving anything in return. Thus, cooperatives may place themselves at a serious disadvantage. They will have forgone attacking the opposing lawyer's position, they will have conceded the weaknesses of their own position, and they will have received no reciprocal value in return. This risk is compounded by the apparent inability of some cooperatives—when facing a skilled competitive negotiator—to recognize the true situation and how one-sided the negotiation has been until it is too late.

Some lawyers argue that cooperative lawyers should not fear looking weak early in a negotiation because it induces tough opponents to overplay their hands and expose their strategy. Professor Williams maintains that this argument, however, is not a good one because of the three "costs" this approach entails: (1) a loss of image, (2) a loss of position, and (3) a loss of negotiating currency.

First, this approach involves a *loss of image.* Competitive negotiators interpret cooperation as a sign of weakness. From their viewpoint, people who are strong and who have strong cases do not make unilateral concessions or admit weaknesses. When negotiators act cooperatively toward them, competitive negotiators actually increase their level of demands and expectations about what they will be able to obtain in the case.

Second, this approach involves a *loss of position.* Once cooperative lawyers have made concessions, it is extremely difficult to take them back. To regain lost ground will be awkward, time-consuming, and sometimes impossible.

Third, this approach involves a *loss of currency.* Concessions are a form of currency. Much of the negotiating process involves submitting and considering offers and making concessions. In this process, negotiators must have something to trade. This reality explains why many negotiators establish initially extreme positions—to create currency to trade. If too many concessions are made too early in the negotiation, cooperative negotiators may be left with no currency to trade when the tough opponent is finally ready to compromise.

3. THE COMPETITIVE STYLE

This subsection discusses the basic elements and dynamics of the competitive style—how this pattern of legal negotiation works and what specifically determines its effectiveness or ineffectiveness. It also discusses the risks or dangers of this style.

a. Basic Elements

The underlying dynamic of the competitive style is *to move psychologically against opponents by word or action*. The tactics of competitive lawyers include high opening demands, few concessions, exaggeration, ridicule, threat, aggression, and accusation. They take a gamesmanship ("poker game") attitude toward legal negotiations. This approach creates high levels of tension and pressure on opponents.

The effect of these tactics on party perceptions is crucial to the success of the style. In psychological terms, the toughness and intimidation of competitive attorneys work on the emotions of the opposing party—causing opponents to become preoccupied with emotional issues and to lose sight of the objective merits of the case. This approach is thus a manipulative one. If these competitive tactics are used effectively, opponents will lose confidence in themselves and their case, will reduce their expectations of what they will be able to obtain in the case, and will accept less than they otherwise would as a settlement outcome.

b. Effective Competitives

According to Professor Williams' research, effective competitive negotiators are seen as *dominating, competitive, forceful, tough, aggressive,* and *uncooper-*

ative. They make *high opening demands.* Research suggests that effective competitive negotiators are able to establish the credibility of high demands by convincing legal argumentation. They use *threats,* are *willing to stretch the facts* in favor of their clients' positions, *stick to their positions,* and are *parsimonious with information about the case.* They sometimes create "false issues" (making a dramatic commitment to an issue that they actually do not consider important) to generate negotiating currency—allowing them to concede that issue in exchange for a major concession from an opponent.

Effective competitive negotiators have three principal objectives: (1) they want to maximize the settlement for the client; (2) they want to obtain a profitable fee for themselves; and (3) they want to outdo or outmaneuver their opponents. However, the goal of getting a maximum settlement value for the client means something different to an effective competitive negotiator than to an effective cooperative negotiator. For effective competitive negotiators, the goal includes a reward to self both in monetary terms and in satisfaction from outdoing an opponent.

Rather than seeking an outcome that is fair to both sides, effective competitive negotiators want to outdo the other side and score a clear victory. Cooperatives feel that cases should be objectively evaluated on their merits. Competitive negotiators feel that they should put the best foot forward and try to make the other side think that the other side's weaknesses are bigger than they really are. The competitive approach also lessens the risk of giving away too much too easily. Nonetheless, effective competitive negotiators do compromise—they are *rational*. The secret is that their style is to appear inflexible and irrational to convince their opponents that they will have to accept an agreement mostly on their terms.

The effectiveness of the competitive approach depends on creating enough pressure and tension to induce an emotional reaction and a reduction in expectations in the opposing party. The competitive style, particularly when it is used in complex cases, may produce more favorable outcomes than a cooperative style. But if the pressure is excessive or is maintained too long, the strategy backfires and trial against a vindictive opponent results.

c. *Ineffective Competitives*

Ineffective competitive negotiators are characterized by negative traits. Professor Williams found that they share only one common personality trait with their effective counterpart: both are *egotistical*. Ineffective competitive negotiators are *headstrong, impatient, intolerant, rigid,* and *loud*; they are *greedy, demanding, unreasonable, uncooperative, arrogant,* and *tactless*; they are *complaining, sarcastic,* and *insincere*.

Ineffective competitive negotiators are also *devious, conniving, impulsive, unpredictable,* and *evasive*; they are also *suspicious, distrustful,* and *unskilled at reading their opponents' cues*; they are *rude, hostile, quarrelsome,* and *obstructive*; they are *disinterested in the needs of the opposing attorney and client.* In sum, they are *irritating* and *obnoxious.*

Like their effective counterparts, ineffective competitive negotiators make high opening demands, but they apparently lack the skills to make convincing arguments in support of them. They use a *take-it-or-leave-it* approach and *threats.* However, ineffective competitive negotiators engage in *bluffs*, take one position and refuse to move from it, employ a narrow range of bargaining tactics, and are ineffective trial lawyers. They also lack the perceptive, convincing, analytical, realistic, self-controlled characteristics that effective competitive negotiators display.

Ineffective competitive negotiators exhibit a lack of social skills. Because ineffective cooperative negotiators do not lack social skills and yet are still seen as ineffective negotiators, it appears that regard or disregard of the social graces does not determine a lawyer's effectiveness. Research suggests that forceful persons who have low regard for social amenities may function effectively as legal negotiators if they can show themselves to be perceptive, analytical, realistic, and self-controlled in negotiations. The lack of these latter traits in ineffective competitive negotiators may account for the perception that they are *argumentative, quarrelsome,* and *irritating.*

Ineffective competitive negotiators often resort to bluffs, bullying, and evasive tactics in an effort to mask a lack of skilled preparation. The underlying difference between effective and ineffective competitive negotiators seems to relate to the quality of legal work being performed, including the expertise with which the attorneys have investigated the facts, studied and understood the applicable legal rules, taken a realistic position with respect to the value of the case, and presented their position in ways that other attorneys would accept as being rational, fair, and persuasive (convincing).

It may follow that lawyers who are prepared have little cause to be argumentative, quarrelsome, rude, and hostile. They can go forward on the merits of their position rather than seek advantage by being personally offensive to opposing lawyers or by stalling, bluffing, or quarreling. Even when negotiators are fully prepared, however, recall from Chapter 1(D)(1) that an adversarial approach may be seen as a breach of etiquette and counterproductive in some transactional settings. It may also be inappropriate in some international legal negotiating contexts.

Finally, ineffective competitive negotiators rate extremely low on ethics and trustworthiness. They are seen as *devious* and *conniving*.

d. Dangers of the Competitive Style

Toughness and unilateral commitment in negotiating generate a marked increase in tension and mistrust that may harm interpersonal relations between the negotiators and the parties they represent. Furthermore, when negotiating lawyers are likely to encounter each other on a continuing basis over time, tension and mistrust generated in one case will influence the dynamics and outcomes of later cases against the same opponent. This effect is magnified as a lawyer's reputation becomes known throughout the bar.

The use of threats and personal intimidation creates stress. Studies indicate that stress reduces a negotiator's ability to understand the opponent's ideas, plans, or wishes. One immediate effect is to distort the communication between the negotiators. Studies indicate that when people communicate under conditions of distrust and tension, they tend to overstate the extent of agreement and the extent of disagreement. Thus, competitive negotiators may be led to believe that their opponents are closer to agreement than is, in fact, the case. Such a negotiator, therefore, may go on to the next item on the agenda or, if an agenda has been completed, may seek closure—only to find that their opponents are in serious disagreement and will not commit themselves to the anticipated agreement.

Furthermore, when competitive negotiators wrongly begin to sense agreement in opponents, they will often increase their demands and expectations when it is unjustified. The result may be a complete breakdown in bargaining. At best, substantial effort by both sides will be needed to overcome the misunderstandings that separate them. Because some of the distance between them is illusory, efforts to reduce it are inefficient.

Another consequence of toughness and intimidation is possible damage to the immediate case in terms of trial. When emotions run high and impasse occurs, the offended parties are often filled with righteous indignation at what they consider unfair treatment. Angry opponents retaliate against tough negotiators by working harder and creating as many obstacles as possible.

Professor Williams' study of several hundred Phoenix lawyers demonstrated that the rate of impasse is significantly higher for effective competitive lawyers than for effective cooperative lawyers. Cooperative effective negotiators obtained a settlement agreement in 84% of their cases and went to trial with the remaining 16%. In contrast, competitive effective negotiators settled only 67% of their cases and faced breakdown and trial in 33%, just over double the trial rate of cooperative negotiators.

The same study likewise showed that average competitive negotiators take a substantially higher proportion of their cases to trial than do average cooperatives. Average cooperative negotiators settled 62% of their cases and tried 38%. In contrast, average competitive negotiators settled 50% and tried 50% of their cases.

The relationship of the settlement rate changed, however, for ineffective cooperative and competitive lawyers. Ineffective cooperative negotiators settled 36% of their cases and took 64% of their cases to trial, while competitive ineffective negotiators settled 67% of their cases and took only 33% to trial. One explanation for this difference may be that ineffective cooperatives know that they are too soft and, as a defense, they feel compelled to protect the client by trying the case—a dubious protection, however, given their low ratings on trial effectiveness. But it shifts the apparent primary responsibility from them to the court.

On the other hand, ineffective competitive negotiators depend on bluffs. They are unprepared on the facts or law, and they are not legally astute. They rely on extreme demands, quarrelsomeness, hostility, rudeness, and other ploys to coerce the other side into settlement. If their bluffs do not work (which generally is the case), they face a particularly excruciating problem. As ineffective trial lawyers, if they try the case, they will be publicly exposed as bluffers. Their safest bet is to bluff to the last minute and then cave in.

Nothing is inherently improper with the higher rate of impasses and trials characteristic of the effective and average competitive negotiators. It may be that competitive lawyers obtain higher outcomes on settled cases as a result of their toughness and that a higher trial rate is the price they pay. Trial, however, does impose high costs and missed opportunities for creative, mutually beneficial solutions, and clients whose cases go to trial may be subsidizing clients whose cases settle. These dangers and liabilities of the competitive style may explain why so few lawyers use it effectively.

4. RECOMMENDED "BLENDED" STYLE

Based on his research, Professor Williams concluded that the most effective approach to a legal negotiation in terms of style was a "blended" one. The approach is "to put the best of both [the cooperative and competitive styles] together in an artful and persuasive manner." In his book, *Effective Negotiation and Settlement*, Williams suggests that the overall objective of a negotiator using this "blended" style is to be seen as (1) "cooperative" and (2) "trustworthy" (both drawn from the cooperative style), and, at the same time, (3) "tough" (drawn from the competitive style). Using this style, the negotiator works to convince the opposing side that (1) the negotiator has a strong case and is able to defend it; (2) the opposing side will have to make substantial concessions to resolve the case; and (3) it is in the opposing side's best interest to do so.

Williams recognizes that being "cooperative" and being "tough" are essentially opposites. Williams suggests that this seemingly incompatible combination can be achieved by the following approach. Drawing on the competitive style, negotiators should (1) consciously develop high expectations, (2) open the negotiations with a relatively high level of demands (essentially, the "maximalist" position discussed below in section F), (3) persuasively demonstrate strength of the negotiator's position, and (4) maintain a relatively small rate of concessions in terms of size, number, and frequency. The negotiator must pay special attention to (1) "conceptualizing the case in its strategically most favorable light" and (2) consistently "defending and promoting that conceptualization until the case is finally laid to rest."

In this "blended" style, this toughness is counter-balanced by (1) demonstrating to the opponent that the negotiator is willing "to make meaningful concessions in the measure required to achieve an acceptable outcome," (2) promising "to cooperate to work out the best possible solution," (3) showing an understanding of the other side's needs and problems, and (4) empathizing and sympathizing with the other side's situation. These are essentially "free concessions" that help convince the other side that the negotiator is being cooperative. Furthermore, the negotiator using a blended strategy would avoid the intimidation, bullying, and cajoling characteristic of the competitive style to enhance the appearance of cooperation.

Finally, according to Williams, a negotiator using this "blended" style should be very perceptive and attentive to the negotiation process. Furthermore, as discussed in Chapter 4, the negotiator must be very alert to the tactics used by the opposing side during every negotiation session and take steps to counter those tactics and lessen their effectiveness.

5. UPDATED RESEARCH ON LEGAL NEGOTIATING STYLES

In 2002, Professor Andrea Kupfer Schneider published the results of a study entitled *Shattering Negotiation Myths: Empirical Evidence on the Effectiveness of Negotiation Style* in the *Harvard Negotiation Law Review*. Her study updated Professor Williams' research, discussed in the preceding subsections. Her study sought to reflect (1) the dramatic demographic changes in the bar in which many more lawyers are now females, (2) the widespread negotiation and mediation training law students and lawyers have now received, and (3) other significant developments that have taken place in the legal profession and legal education since Professor Williams conducted his research in 1976.

Using updated rating scales to reflect "modern vocabulary used by negotiation scholars" and a broader demographic base, Professor Schneider's bipolar analysis of her data for two clusters indicated that "the two styles of [legal] negotiation have clearly diverged in the last twenty-five years." Professor Schneider's survey found that only two adjectives describing negotiation *behavior* now overlap between the two basic styles for "effective" legal negotiators: (1) "experienced" and (2) "confident."

Furthermore, the percentage of competitive legal negotiators who were seen as effective in the Williams' study dropped dramatically in her study. At the same time, the percentage of competitive negotiators who were seen as ineffective had increased dramatically. Based on these and other findings, Professor Schneider concluded that "it looks like the gap between these styles is widening. While the . . . cooperative group has remained much the same, the . . . competitive group seems to be growing more extreme and more negative." In addition, as competitive "bargaining has become more extreme, it has also become far less effective. This is a key lesson for those hoping to become effective 'Rambo' negotiators."

In terms of negotiation *goals* (as opposed to descriptions of behavior), Professor Schneider found that effective negotiators, like in the early Williams study, still shared several common goals regardless of style. Effective negotiators were perceived as being interested in the needs of their client, maximizing the settlement for the client, and seeing that the client's needs were met.

In addition, Professor Schneider's study suggested that both types of effective negotiators today are perceived as (1) being "intelligent," (2) "acting consistently with the best interests of their client," (3) "representing their client zealously and within the bounds of the law," and (4) "taking satisfaction in the exercise of legal skills." In sum, according to Professor Schneider, "[t]hey are assertive, smart, and prepared."

With regard to labels, Professor Schneider felt that Williams' "cooperative" label leads lawyers to "make false assumptions about how lawyers were actually described (including descriptors such as maximizing settlement, experienced, rational, and analytical)" in Williams' study and "to assume that cooperative only describes personable push-overs" who are "soft, acquiescent, [and] willing to concede in order to get along." Such lawyers appear to fail to appreciate the differences between effective and ineffective cooperative negotiators and the interplay of strategy with style, particularly problem solving.

D. LEGAL NEGOTIATING STRATEGIES

In addition to adopting a negotiating style (cooperative or competitive), legal negotiators adopt a basic negotiating strategy. In this regard, Self-Test 3 in Chapter 1(G), above, asked you to choose between pairs of descriptions or approaches. These fundamental choices were developed by Professor Carrie Menkel-Meadow. The first item in each of the pairs reflects an "adversarial" strategy. The second item in each of the pairs reflects a "problem-solving" strategy. This section discusses these two fundamentally different strategies and the following section discusses how they interact with legal negotiating styles.

1. ADVERSARIAL STRATEGIES

a. *"Target Points" and "Minimum Dispositions" or "Resistance Points"*

One possible approach to a legal negotiation is for the client and lawyer to set dollar figures—what are often termed a "target point" and a "minimum disposition" or a "resistance point." The target point reflects what the client hopes to achieve. The minimum disposition or resistance point reflects the least favorable settlement that the client is willing to accept—often referred to as the "bottom line" below which the client is willing to reach an impasse or deadlock.

The combination of the negotiating parties' minimum dispositions or resistance points establishes the "bargaining range" of all possible outcomes between the two respective resistance points. Assume, for example, that the plaintiff's minimum disposition (resistance point) and target point are $60,000 and $90,000 and that the defendant's target point and minimum disposition (resistance point) are $50,000 and \$75,000. The bargaining range is between \$60,000 and \$75,000:

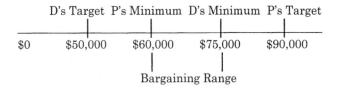

At the negotiating sessions, each side presents its "position" in the form of offers and counteroffers. Typically, the parties argue the "merits" of the positions. They continue to make additional offers and counteroffers until either an agreement is reached or a deadlock occurs.

Professor Menkel-Meadow points out that the target and resistance points are generally set in terms of fungible commodities, usually money. Items that are not readily quantifiable, such as pain and suffering, are converted to monetary amounts, added to other monetary amounts, and are treated as fungible items on the negotiating continuum. The parties work toward a negotiated result through a pattern of offers, counteroffers, and concessions. This strategic approach to legal negotiation is essentially "linear." Movement along the line reflects a win/loss game in which one party's gain is the other party's loss.

This adversarial strategy reflects what bargaining theorists call a "zero-sum game," in which the losses equal the winnings. Its basic goal is to maximize the gain by the party employing it ("winning or gaining unilateral advantage") and the resulting balance sheet always equals zero. In effect, the parties are dividing up a "fixed pie" of resources. What one side gains, the other side loses.

Trial verdicts are an example of a zero-sum game (except when there is an imbalance in the costs of prosecuting the case, which means that one party may have paid grossly more than the other regardless of which side won or lost). Other examples of zero-sum games include athletic contests (in which one team or person wins and the other loses) and hiring quotas. Distributional methods (zero-sum) are often viewed as being "inefficient" because they are not good at loss allocation. They give an all-or-nothing solution and tend to create highly contentious ("adversarial") negotiations.

b. Influence of Case Evaluation and "Form Contracts" in an Adversarial Negotiation

Legal rights and remedies enforceable in court provide the framework for negotiated settlement of civil legal disputes. If the defendant refuses to negotiate and settle on satisfactory terms, the plaintiff may be able to obtain compensation or other relief from the defendant through a legally enforceable judgment or order from a court of law. Because negotiation in civil litigation is ordinarily viewed against this backdrop of trial outcome, predicting the trial outcome of a given case plays an important role for many negotiators in setting initial negotiation positions, and setting minimum dispositions, target points, and evaluating the reasonableness of settlement offers.

Thus, as aptly pointed out by Professor Menkel-Meadow, negotiators adopting an adversarial strategy appear to be strongly influenced by what has been termed the "shadow of the law" in a litigational setting. Similarly, in a transactional setting, the negotiators appear to be strongly influenced by the "shadow of the form contract." Lawyers using an adversarial strategy often think in limited terms—what the court would award in terms of damages or injunctive relief or the traditional form provision or common business practice—even though other more creative or unusual provisions would better serve the parties' particular interests and needs.

As discussed in the next subsections of this chapter, the traditional argumentative nature of discussion and posturing ("competitive reactive dynamics") may, in turn, inhibit the search for finding creative solutions. As Fisher and Ury in *Getting to Yes: Negotiating Agreement Without Giving In* aptly indicate, the resulting "tug-of-war" becomes in large measure "a contest of will." It often seems that this process reflects what Charles Dickens noted long ago in *Bleak House*: "No two lawyers can talk for five minutes without coming to total disagreement."

c. *"Best Alternative to a Negotiated Agreement" ("BATNA")*

Instead of focusing on a minimum disposition, Fisher and Ury suggest that the focus should be on the "Best Alternative to a Negotiated Agreement" ("BATNA")—the best result that each party can achieve if the negotiated agreement is not reached. In the personal injury, plea bargain, and other litigation contexts, the BATNA for each party should reflect a realistic appraisal of possible litigated outcomes. A meaningful statement of probable trial outcome (BATNA) in this context is one of the most important pieces of information that a client needs in order to make an informed decision about whether to offer or accept a settlement of the case. It is not very useful to a client in making a decision about settlement for you to say, as stated on one client counseling videotape, for example, "You have a good case, but trial, of course, is always a crap shoot."

To the extent possible, descriptive and mathematical language of probable outcomes will usually be more meaningful. For example, legal negotiators might term their evaluation in this way: "I would say that you have a strong case. I think you will be a good witness and would be liked by the jury. Although it is difficult to predict, at this point I estimate that you have a seventy-five percent chance of winning a verdict of $50,000 at trial. There is a slim possibility that the verdict might go as high as $75,000 or that you might recover as little as $15,000 or even less. The defendant has offered $40,000 to settle this case. The real question is whether you are willing to take what is certain—the $40,000—or want to try to get more at trial but with the risk you might get less."

In a transactional setting, the BATNA reflects an analysis of all possible alternatives—for example, the price at which the buyer could obtain the item from another seller or the cost of fabricating the item internally. By assessing how realistic those alternatives are, a negotiator and the client can determine what the best alternatives to a negotiated agreement are for each party. Such an analysis will help a negotiator frame realistic expectations about what the other party would be willing to accept. It will also help prevent a negotiator from being pressured or duped into an unfavorable settlement and, in fact, make a negotiator more able to affect the results of the negotiation.

2. INTEREST-BASED, "PROBLEM-SOLVING" (INTEGRATIVE) STRATEGIES

a. *The Parties' Underlying Interests and Needs*

One risk of setting a minimum disposition and taking firm dollar "positions" at an early point with a client is that it can create unrealistic expectations in light of developments, counterarguments, and new information that may come to light during discovery, research, investigation, and negotiation. Inflexible minimum dispositions and positions also inhibit creative solutions.

Fisher and Ury point out that knowing a client's goals (interests, needs, values, and concerns) helps a negotiator know what to bargain for. It also assists a negotiator in making tradeoffs based on the relative importance of the goals to the client. For example, in the personal injury context, the client's needs and interests might be to have all medical bills paid, to have a stream of income to meet living expenses, and to have sufficient funds to meet special needs (similar to the possibilities reflected in a structured settlement discussed below). By focusing on a minimum disposition and positions rather than each party's needs and interests, the negotiators may miss the opportunity to develop a settlement that meets each party's needs and interests and maximizes each party's benefits.

In an interest-based, problem-solving approach to negotiation, the key is *why* someone *wants* something. The oft-told story of two sisters with one orange illustrates this point. In the story, both sisters wanted the orange. They negotiated over who should get the orange. They reached a distributive solution to satisfy their stated desires by cutting it in half. The first sister squeezed her half for the juice and threw away the peel. The second sister grated the peel from her half for a cake and threw away the rest, including the juice. Both *wanted* the orange. However, each *needed* (or had an "interest" in) only the juice or the peel. Both of their interests could have been satisfied with part of the whole orange. Thus, they could have maximized their gain (without detriment to the other).

Thus, the parties' stated "demands" will often mask several needs and interests. Usually, those underlying needs and interests will not be exactly the same. Nor will they necessarily conflict. Needs and interests run the full range of possibilities—from approval to freedom to honor to physical needs to economic well-being. Identifying the parties' interests often opens up the realm of possible solutions from a single-based solution (position) to a variety of options that have the effect of "expanding the pie."

Prior to entering a negotiation, a negotiator should carefully identify what the client wants, the likely objectives of the other party or parties to the transaction, the points of leverage that each party may have, and the acceptable alternatives to accomplishing the parties' respective goals. Clients and their lawyers sometimes fail to realize that the clients' objectives may be accomplished in a variety of ways. Some of the equally acceptable alternatives may have substantially varying value to the other party or parties to the transaction.

Professor Carrie Menkel-Meadow in her article, *Toward Another View of Legal Negotiation: The Structure of Problem Solving*, suggests the following useful framework for inquiring into the needs and objectives of the parties. Quoted below by permission are her questions illustrating the type of concerns that should be considered in each of the categories:

Economic Needs and Objectives (including transaction costs). What are the monetary requirements now—compensation, return on investment, liquidity for payment? What might be the future monetary needs? What is the money needed for? Are there any cheaper means available? Are there cash substitutes that are available and acceptable? What are the tax consequences of payment/receipt now? Later? What payment structure is desirable—lump sum, installments? Why? What are the transaction costs or solution costs of negotiation as opposed to litigation?

Legal Issues. What legal regulations govern the parties' situation? Must there be an admission of liability? Is a legal judgment necessary? Why? Is a formal document evidencing agreement desirable or required? What are the likely future legal consequences of actions taken? What are the parties likely to do if one of them breaches an agreement? What assets will be available in the future for legal action, if necessary?

Social Considerations and Relationships. What are the social needs of the parties? How do others feel about this dispute or transaction? Will family members, friends, business associates, employers, employees be affected by actions taken by the parties? If not affected now, how will any of these people feel if things change in the future?

Psychological Considerations (including feelings and risk aversion). What are the psychological needs of the parties? Does one desire vindication, retribution, power? Why? What will be the long-term psychological consequences of satisfying or not satisfying these needs? How risk averse are the parties? What are their motivations for pursuing their aims in the negotiation? How might some of these feelings change if they forgo litigation now or if they insist on obtaining some advantage?

Ethical and Moral Considerations. How fair do the parties desire to be with each other? What are the consequences of acting altruistically or dishonestly now? In the future? Will there be feelings of guilt later for "taking advantage" of the other side?

Clients may also fail to consider or articulate other needs and interests that will have unrealized potential consequences. Professor Menkel-Meadow points out that these latent needs and concerns can often be ascertained by following up and by asking "why" a particular item, thing, or outcome is desired. Furthermore, legal negotiators consider how these needs and objectives may change over time—in other words, both in the short term and the long run. Likewise, the lawyer should be willing to probe the legitimacy and propriety of particular goals, if appropriate.

b. *Interest-Based, "Problem Solving"*

An interest-based, "problem-solving" strategy reflects what bargaining theorists would call a "non-zero-sum game." The classic example of a non-zero-sum game is the "Prisoner's Dilemma," in which two suspects are being held by the police. Each suspect is going to be interviewed separately by the prosecuting attorney, who will try to convince each, in turn, to testify for the state in return for a lighter sentence. Both prisoners know the following: (1) if one of them confesses and the other does not, the one who confesses will be given lenient treatment while the one who refuses to confess will receive a severe sentence; (2) if both prisoners confess, they both will receive moderate rather than severe sentences; and (3) if neither confesses, they both will receive light sentences.

In this situation, a defendant is likely to envision the *worst possible* result involved in the defendant's choices (confess = moderate sentence; not confess = severe punishment). From this perspective, each defendant is likely to confess, which guarantees that the severe punishment will be avoided—and, if both confess, forecloses the possibility that a light sentence will be obtained. Thus, in absence of mutual trust and cooperation, the best that they can achieve is a compromise moderate sentence. If they could cooperate, they could achieve a better mutual outcome by not confessing and receiving light sentences.

This approach, which involves examining goals and presenting alternative solutions, is known as "integrative bargaining" or "problem solving." By discovering and evaluating the various alternatives in light of the interests of the parties and by arranging those alternatives, this approach seeks to find a package solution that yields benefit to both sides. The central emphasis under this approach involves skill in evaluating the value to each party of the alternatives and combining them in the most profitable manner. Agreement is reached by efficient trade-offs and creative beneficial solutions.

Consider the following simple example. Assume that Airline *A* and Passenger *B* are having a dispute over alleged abusive treatment of *B* by Airline *A's* personnel. *B* claims to have suffered emotional distress from the treatment. Instead of paying *B* a sum of money, *A* could provide *B* with a written apology and free travel (subject to the normal frequent-flyer, capacity-control restrictions). In this way, *B* receives vindication (the apology) and the equivalent of a substantial sum of money (free travel). On the other hand, the apology costs *A* virtually nothing to prepare, and the seats occupied by *B* could well have been unsold. Furthermore, by encouraging *B* to continue to travel on their flights, the airline has an opportunity to re-establish good will with *B* and secure *B's* future business.

Thus, as Fisher and Ury point out, the key to creating value out of the parties' differences is matching what is low cost to one party with what is high in benefit to the other party and vice versa. Professor Menkel-Meadow suggests that the following areas for potential mutual gains can be explored:

(1) *what* could be distributed;

(2) *when* it could be distributed;

(3) *by whom* it could be distributed;

(4) *how* it could be distributed; and

(5) *how much* of it could be distributed.

Some lawyers see integrative bargaining or problem-solving negotiation as having limited utility in a personal injury action in which the fundamental issue is how much money the defendant is going to pay the plaintiff (a distributive problem). Nonetheless, even when only money is at issue, important integrative elements may be involved, such as when the money is paid (use value of money, effect of inflation, and immediate needs of the parties), tax effects, and whether payment can be partially or totally made in kind instead of cash. Furthermore, as Professor Menkel-Meadow points out, focusing on the underlying *use* of the money will enliven the problem-solving process.

To use some of her examples, suppose that the plaintiff in a personal injury case wants money to purchase an automobile. In this situation, the defendant might be able to supply an automobile at a lower cost than the market price that the defendant would have to pay in settlement. Numerous other examples could be given to illustrate that the parties to a negotiation do not necessarily value the fixed resource equally. Similarly, it may be less costly to the defendant to provide the plaintiff with employment, and thus earnings, to satisfy the plaintiff's rehabilitation needs (instead of money to purchase rehabilitation services on the open market).

E. COMBINATIONS OF STYLES AND STRATEGIES

The division of "styles" from "strategies" in the preceding section was developed by Bastress and Harbaugh in their book, *Interviewing, Counseling, and Negotiation: Skills for Effective Representation.* Working with Professor Menkel-Meadow's graphic format and basic concepts, Bastress and Harbaugh present the following conception of the possible combinations of strategy and style:

(1) adversarial, competitive bargainers;

(2) cooperative adversarial bargainers;

(3) competitive problem solvers; and

(4) cooperative problem solvers.

	ADVERSARIAL STRATEGY	**PROBLEM-SOLVING STRATEGY**
COMPETITIVE STYLE	Rigid positions, Hard bargaining	Limited consideration of needs, solutions
COOPERATIVE STYLE	Concessions and Compromise	Open consideration of needs, solutions

Competitive and cooperative adversarials conceive the negotiation process in "linear" terms, as described in the preceding sections. On the other hand, competitive and cooperative "problem solvers" focus on the parties' interests and creating resources rather than "characterizing issues as fungible commodities along a continuum."

However, in contrast to cooperative problem-solvers, Bastress and Harbaugh point out that competitive problem solvers tend to be less open in articulating the needs of the parties and may try to manipulate the characterization of those needs by advancing feigned needs and discounting legitimate needs of other parties. In addition, unlike cooperative problem solvers, who truly try to maximize the joint and mutual gains of the parties, competitive problem solvers may not willingly discuss all potential solutions because they do not give their client a "positive advantage." Despite the *appearance* of being deeply concerned about the opponent's benefits, such a competitive negotiator may have little regard for the gains and losses of the other party. As Bastress and Harbaugh conclude, from the competitive problem solver's perspective, "[i]f the opponent prospers, so be it; if the opponent is unsuccessful, so be it."

Professor Schneider's study published in 2002, which updated Professor Williams' earlier research and which was discussed above, likewise found four combinations of style and strategy. Using a four cluster analysis on her data, Professor Schneider found the following natural groupings: (1) 38% were "true problem-solving negotiators"; (2) 27% were "cautious problem solvers"; (3) 21.5% were "ethical adversarial negotiators"; and (4) 12.5% were "unethical adversarial negotiators."

The top adjectives for these four identifiable clusters clearly identify their respective styles. The true problem solvers were seen as *ethical, experienced, personable, trustworthy, rational, fair-minded, agreeable, communicative, realistic, accommodating, perceptive, confident, sociable, self-controlled, adaptable, dignified, helpful, astute, poised,* and *flexible.*

Like the true problem solvers, the cautious problem solvers were seen as *ethical, experienced, personable, self-controlled, confident, rational, agreeable,* and *dignified,* but lacked the other distinguishing characteristics of true problem solvers listed above. Although in somewhat different priorities, both the true problem solvers and the cautious problem solvers had similar goals: ethical conduct, fair settlement, maximizing settlement, meeting interests of both sides, avoiding litigation, meeting client's needs, maintaining good relations with the opposing negotiator, using legal skills well, maintaining good relations between the parties, improving reputation with the opposing negotiator (in the case of the true problem solvers) or for the firm (in the case of the cautious problem solvers), and obtaining a profitable fee.

With regard to the ethical and unethical adversarial groups, although many of the descriptions overlapped, their order differed. The top five adjectives in the ethical group were *confident* (eighteenth in the unethical group), *assertive* (ninth in the unethical group), *arrogant* (sixth in the unethical group), *headstrong* (third in the unethical group and the only one to overlap in the top five list for each category), and *experienced* (which was not listed for the unethical group). Furthermore, unlike the unethical group, "the ethical group was *not* described as manipulative, conniving, deceptive, evasive, complaining, rude, angry, intolerant, sarcastic, greedy, or stern."

In sum, unlike those in the ethical adversarial group, the unethical adversarial negotiators were *unpleasant* (*i.e., discourteous, unfriendly*, and *tactless*); they were *untrustworthy* (*i.e., insincere, devious, dishonest*, and *distrustful*); they were *uninterested in the client or lawyer on the other side* (*i.e., no understanding of the opposing client, unconcerned how opposing counsel would look, no consideration of opposing counsel's needs*, and *unconcerned about the needless infliction of harm*); they were *inflexible in their view of the case and their strategies* (*i.e., narrow view of case, rigid, took one position, narrow range of strategies, focused on a single solution, fixed concept of negotiation*); they were *manipulative* (*i.e.*, *attacked, used take-it-or-leave-it, inaccurate case estimate,* and *advanced unwarranted claims*); and, finally, they were *uncooperative* and *unreasonable* as well as viewed their negotiation as *"win-lose"* and *obstructed* the negotiation. In contrast, the ethical adversarial group had a broader view of the case and were more pleasant.

Importantly, Professor Schneider found that among these groups, the true problem solvers had the largest percentage of negotiators considered to be effective (72%) and the fewest ineffective negotiators (1%), along with 27% rated as average. Twenty-four percent of the cautious problem solvers were considered to be effective while 64% were rated as average and 12% were rated as ineffective. In contrast, 75% of the unethical adversarial group were considered ineffective while 22% were rated as average and only 2.5% were considered effective. With regard to the ethical adversarial negotiators, 40% were considered ineffective, 44% were average, and only 16% were rated as effective. As Professor Schneider aptly concludes, "[w]hen lawyers are able to maximize their problem-solving skills balancing assertiveness and empathy, they are more effective on behalf of their clients" and "are able to enlarge the pie through creativity and flexibility."

Other commentators have used different terminology and classify the basic strategies in different ways, sometimes intermixed with elements of style. Fisher and Ury in *Getting to Yes: Negotiating Agreement Without Giving In*, for example, refer to (1) hard, (2) soft, and (3) principled strategies. In their book *Beyond Winning: Negotiating to Create Value in Deals and Disputes*, Mnookin, Peppet, and Tulumello outline four types of behavior: (1) accommodating, (2) avoiding, (3) competing, and (4) problem-solving. Lax and Sebenius categorize negotiation strategies as (1) value-claiming and (2) value-creating.

In their book *Social Conflict: Escalation, Stalemate, and Settlement*, Pruitt and Rubin describe the following strategies: (1) contending; (2) problem solving; (3) yielding; (4) inactivity; and (5) withdrawal. Pruitt and Rubin describe a "Dual Concerns Model" as a predictor of which of these strategies a negotiator will adopt. The dual concerns reflect (a) concern about the outcome of one's own side and (b) concern about the outcome of the other side—in terms of each side's needs and interests. According to this model, the balance and strength of these concerns will dictate the strategy. For instance, a high concern for mutual outcomes will encourage the adoption of a problem-solving strategy. On the other hand, a strong concern for the outcome of one's own side will engender a contending strategy while a strong concern for the outcome of the other side will encourage a yielding strategy. Weak concern or indifference toward both parties' outcomes will encourage inactivity.

No matter how the combination of styles and strategies are described, however, the best of mix of styles and strategies should always reflect the basic type of legal negotiation involved—civil disputes, contractual transactions, labor-management negotiations, criminal cases, divorce and domestic relations problems, and international legal negotiations. As discussed out in Chapter 1(D), above, each of these types of legal negotiations reflects a specialized kind of negotiation involving different customs, practices, and peculiarities.

In this regard, a good legal negotiator carefully takes into account two critical factors: (1) the extent to which the parties perceive the existence of continuing relationship for themselves and (2) the extent to which the negotiation involves voluntary exchanges as opposed to civil disputes, for example, in which the parties have enforceable legal rights and remedies if the parties do not reach a mutually satisfactory agreement outside of court.

F. STAGES OF LEGAL NEGOTIATIONS

Many commentators have observed that negotiation of lawsuits is a repetitive process involving identifiable and reasonably predictable patterns. For example, in *A Practical Guide to Negotiation*, Thomas F. Guernsey usefully breaks the negotiation process down into ten distinct stages: (1) preparation and planning; (2) ice breaking; (3) agenda control; (4) information bargaining; (5) proposals, offers, and demands; (6) persuasion and justification; (7) concessions and reformulation; (8) crisis resulting in either resolution or deadlock; (9) closing; and (10) memorialization.

Like descriptions of style and strategy, however, individual commentators do not use common terminology to describe these processes. Generally speaking, some commentators emphasize functional aspects while others focus on patterns of activity.

The following summary and discussion divides the dynamics of the legal negotiation process into four distinct stages. This description follows the patterns described by Professor Gerald Williams in his book, *Legal Negotiation and Settlement*:

STAGE	ACTIVITY
STAGE ONE: ORIENTATION & POSITIONING	1. Working relationship established 2. Initial negotiating positions adopted
STAGE TWO: ARGUMENTATION	1. Argument and persuasion 2. Search for alternative solutions 3. Concession making
STAGE THREE: EMERGENCE & CRISIS	1. Pressure for agreement or deadlock builds 2. Crisis occurs
STAGE FOUR: AGREEMENT OR FINAL BREAKDOWN	1. Deadlock or basic agreement occurs 2. Wrap up details 3. Formalize agreement

The above chart and the following discussion reflect the traditional adversarial conception of the negotiation process. Intermixed with this discussion will be commentary on the problem-solving strategy and other functional aspects of the negotiation process. This structure primarily reflects a litigational context. Similar functional considerations, however, arise in a transactional contexts in which the lawyers prepare for the negotiation, exchange and assess information, work for solutions, use persuasion, and work toward closure or deadlock.

No matter how they are described, however, it is readily apparent that lawyers sometimes fail to recognize the negotiating patterns. Their attention and energy are often focused on the details of the pretrial litigation and trial preparation. Inexperienced lawyers often misperceive which stage of the process the case is in and use tactics that are unnecessary or even harmful to the dynamics of the negotiation. One example is the tendency of some lawyers to move psychologically through the stages more quickly than a tough opponent; then when no agreement is forthcoming, they assume that the final stage has been reached and precipitate a final breakdown in the negotiations.

1. STAGE ONE: ORIENTATION AND POSITIONING

Stage One involves two related dynamics: orientation and positioning. During this initial stage, the opposing lawyers begin dealing with each other, and they establish their opening positions. They also undertake several basic litigation tasks during this stage. These tasks include filing suit, researching the factual and legal elements of the case, and assessing the "value" of the case based on the strengths and weaknesses that become apparent. During this process, the "competitive" lawyers may attempt to establish a position of dominance that carries over into the later stages. To the extent that the case is discussed during this stage, the lawyers tend to talk primarily about the strengths or merits of their side of the case—often in very general terms.

a. Orientation

As they begin to work on a case, the lawyers must interact. The lawyers may exchange letters and litigation documents, make phone calls to each other, and conduct discovery. During these interactions, each lawyer naturally becomes oriented to the basic approach and style of the other. The preexisting reputations of the lawyers and their prior negotiating experiences and other dealings with each other also influence this orientation process.

The relationship that emerges is an important factor in determining how the negotiators will approach each other and what strategies and tactics will be used. The preparation of each lawyer and general level of their legal skills will be gauged. Some lawyers will try to establish a position of dominance during this period by using intimidating tactics and toughness (which will foreshadow further use of this approach in later stages). Some lawyers will try to establish their status by conveying information about their experience and educational background, and by using other subtle techniques, such as name dropping. Likewise, communication patterns, elements of trustworthiness, and other aspects of the relations between the lawyers develop.

In a transactional setting, Professor Norbert Jacker suggests that part of the negotiator's preparation should be to find out as much as possible about the other negotiator or negotiators who will be involved. This background information might include where they went to school, what type of law practice they have, how busy they are, their experience, and other information that will give insight into their likely strategy and style. This type of information can also be pursued during the course of casual conservation.

b. *Positioning*

Another basic aspect of Stage One is that many lawyers come forward with an opening position. During Stage One, negotiators using an adversarial approach seek to create the illusion of being inalterably committed to their opening positions. Professor Williams points out that this tactic serves several purposes. First, it lends credibility to the demand, and, particularly when the demand is a relatively high one, it gives time for the demand to have its effect on the hopes or expectations of the other side. Second, it gives each negotiator time to make further evaluations of the value of the case and to gain information about what the other side is willing to accept. Third, when the negotiators are ready to begin more serious negotiation, they are better informed and better able to bargain than when the extreme demands were established.

In developing their respective positions, negotiators face uncertainties: the facts are not fully known, the legal questions are not fully researched, and unforeseen developments may loom on the horizon. In the face of these uncertainties, negotiators typically leave themselves a certain amount of latitude. The basic approaches fall into the following categories: "maximalist" (or "extreme") demands, "equitable" (or "moderate") demands, and "integrative" ("problem-solving") proposals.

Some lawyers take a maximalist position, which involves asking for more—sometimes much more— than the lawyer expects to obtain. According to Professor Williams, maximalist positioning has four principal advantages. First, it avoids the danger of committing to an overly modest evaluation of the case. Second, it effectively hides a negotiator's real or minimum expectations, and thus it provides a cover while the negotiator seeks to learn an opponent's real position. Third, it creates currency—something with which to make concessions. This currency may be especially important when the opponent has also opened with a corresponding high (low) demand. Fourth, it may increase the likelihood of a higher outcome, when coupled with an effective strategy. Studies indicate that bargainers unsure of the value of the case tend to use the opponent's opening bid to set their own goals. Thus, against some opponents, maximalist positioning may influence the opposing side's expectations. It also enhances settlement value because it raises the mid-point and thus ties in the "natural" psychological tendency to settle near the midpoint of the initial positions.

On the other hand, Professor Williams points out that maximalist positioning has two principal disadvantages. First, it may enhance the risk of breakdown and trial. Competent opponents will prefer the extra burden of trial to the unreasonable demands and accompanying tactics of a maximalist negotiator. Second, if the demand is "too high," it may lose its effectiveness because it may be interpreted as evidence of unreasonableness—damaging the maximizer's credibility. It is particularly harmful against opponents who have a good idea of the value of the case. They use the opponent's opening offer to assess the reasonableness of the opponent's goals.

In specific instances, several factors will influence how high a demand can be without losing its effectiveness. One factor is the nature of the action. For example, by their nature, contract damages are less inflatable than personal injury damages. Another factor is local custom or specialized practice. Specialized groups within the bar develop norms and customs that provide measures against which the reasonableness or extremism of a demand can be evaluated. Some demands thus lack credibility on their face by inappropriateness and lack of congruity in the context in which they are made.

According to Professor Williams, an equitable position is one calculated to be fair to both (or all) sides. The advantage of equitable positioning is that it may create a lower risk of breakdown and deadlock than a maximalist approach. It also is viewed as the most economical and efficient method of conflict resolution because it avoids the costs of delay occasioned by extreme bargaining positions.

Equitable positioners reason that it is out of trust that negotiators make concessions. If that trust is not rewarded or returned in a fair fashion, further concessions should be withheld until the opponent reciprocates. Furthermore, under this view, until both sides come forward with reasonable opening positions, equitable positioners would consider the case unready for serious negotiation. In this context, the goal of the maximalist would be to convince the equitable positioner that the maximalist's position is a reasonable one.

In general, equitable positioners do not open the negotiations with a statement specifying their final view of the ultimate fair solution. Rather they open with a position which demonstrates that they are serious about finding agreement. They work toward a mid-point between their reasonable opening position and the reasonable opening position of their opponent. Of course, they face the risk of moving toward a high mid-point if they are effectively convinced of the possibility that the maximalist outcome is possible, given a particular scenario—perfect jury, characterization of facts, and the uncertainties of the case.

As discussed in the preceding section, integrative positioning and subsequent integrative, problem-solving bargaining involve presenting several alternative solutions in light of the parties' needs and concerns. This approach seeks to find a package solution that yields non-zero-sum benefit to both sides. Integrative positioning and problem-solving bargaining involve assessing the value to each party of the alternatives, working to expand the total resources available for exchange by the parties, and combining them in a profitable manner. This approach is widely regarded as especially useful when the parties to a legal dispute depend upon each other to avoid a mutually destructive outcome. It is also often identified with exchange transactions involving many variables and multi-party disputes.

c. *Duration of Stage One*

When litigation is involved, current patterns among lawyers show that Stage One generally continues over a longer period of time than all of the other stages combined—ordinarily months or years. At least one reason for this long period is that in many actionable legal disputes the lawyers do not begin seriously considering settlement until trial deadlines make themselves felt—which often does not happen for two years or more.

Empirical data showing litigation and settlement patterns in Phoenix, Arizona, collected by Professor Williams suggest that deadline pressures are perceived differently in each specialized area of law. For example, in personal injury cases, 42.5% were settled from two to ten days before trial; only 2.5% of personal injury cases that settled held out until the day of trial. The pattern is even more extreme in criminal cases. Over 32% of the criminal cases were not resolved until the day of trial. An additional 35.5% were settled from two to ten days before trial; the remainder settled from eleven to ninety days before trial.

In contrast, in commercial and real property disputes, the mere threat of filing suit may be considered heavy handed: 35% of the real property disputes and 29% of the commercial disputes were settled without filing suit. Furthermore, when suit is filed in commercial and real property cases, the deadline pressures begin to mount two months or more before trial. In commercial cases, for example, 4.5% settled the day of the trial, only 12.5% settled two to ten days before trial, and the bulk of cases settled from eleven to sixty days before trial.

In light of these varying perceptions of deadline pressures, Professor Williams suggests that lawyers should adjust their own expectations and sensitivities accordingly. For example, lawyers handling personal injury suits who feel an intense need to settle two months before trial are likely to be doing their clients and themselves a disservice if they overreact to the approach of the trial date.

2. STAGE TWO: ARGUMENTATION, COMPROMISE, AND SEARCH FOR ALTERNATIVE SOLUTIONS

Stage Two commences when the serious settlement discussions begin. During this stage, large amounts of information are often exchanged. Negotiators taking an adversarial approach will try to present this information in the strategically most favorable light. During this argumentation process, the legal and factual issues become more clearly defined, and the strengths and weaknesses of each side become more apparent. The negotiators adjust their assessments of the best alternatives to a negotiated agreement, minimum dispositions, and target points. At the same time, negotiators taking an adversarial approach will attempt to gather information about the real or hidden expectations of the other side without disclosing information about their own minimum expectations and utilities. An important aspect of this argumentation process is that each side's initial expectations may undergo substantial changes in light of the presentations. Indeed, the amount of change and the direction of the change depends, in large part, on each negotiator's advocacy and bargaining skills.

It is usually in Stage Two that the first concessions are made. Concessions are important devices because they are the primary means by which agreement can be approached. They also have importance as instruments of strategy. One problem that the negotiator faces is predicting and assessing the effect of making a concession in an adversarial context. For example, concession making may become reciprocal, in which one concession will be met by concessions of a similar magnitude by the other side. On the other hand, concession making by one negotiator may be met by unresponsive behavior. In fact, with certain types of opponents, if further concessions are made without inducing reciprocal ones, making those additional concessions will actually cause opponents to use progressively more aggressive and demanding tactics and to upgrade the opposing side's expectations.

A negotiator using a problem-solving approach will attempt to provide information about the client's underlying concerns and needs. Fisher and Ury suggest that negotiators using a problem-solving approach should spend time establishing the legitimacy of their clients' interests. If the opposing negotiator attempts to pattern the process into traditional positional bargaining—offer, counteroffer, concessions, threats, and warnings—the negotiator using the problem-solving approach should probe the opposing negotiator's positions to learn information about the opposing party's underlying interests and needs through the use of "why" questions. Fisher and Ury urge a negotiator following a problem-solving approach to listen actively and to acknowledge openly the other side's needs, interests, and concerns. The emphasis should be on identifying interests and needs and solving the problem. The negotiators and their clients generate possible solutions. When both negotiators take a cooperative problem-solving approach, the sessions may take on more of what is called a "brainstorming" or collaborative atmosphere.

Professor Donald Gifford in his article, *The Synthesis of Legal Counseling and Negotiation Models: Preserving Client-Centered Advocacy in the Negotiation Context*, points out that most legal negotiations occur over an extended period of time rather than a single negotiation session. These encounters may take place in unplanned, informal discussions, telephone contacts, written correspondence, and face-to-face negotiating sessions. During this extended time, there will be several interchanges between the lawyers, intermixed with meetings between the lawyers and their respective clients. It is thus an "on-going *cyclical* process." In this context, good communication with the client is essential. Lawyers should continually re-assess with the client factual and legal developments, the client's possibly changing interests, and new information gained about the opposing party's concerns and interests. In particular, the client's BATNA and priorities may change.

3. STAGE THREE: EMERGENCE AND CRISIS

As Stage Two continues, the negotiators come under pressure of approaching deadlines. At some point, each side taking an adversarial approach realizes that one or both of them must make major concessions, present new alternatives, or admit deadlock and resort to trial. This realization commences Stage Three. During this stage, each side seeks and gives clues about areas in which concessions might be made. New alternatives are proposed and concessions are made. Finally, a crisis is reached in which neither side wants to give any more. Both sides are wary of being exploited. Both sides perhaps have given up more than they would like. Both sides know they must stop somewhere. The deadline is upon them. At this point, under the traditional adversarial bargaining, one party makes a "final" offer.

This final demand presents to the opposing negotiator the classic threefold choice: take it, leave it, or come up with something else. If the other's final offer is flatly rejected, a breakdown and impasse occurs. Professor Williams points out that the third alternative, to come up with something else, does not have to be a significant concession. It can be an integrative, problem-solving proposal involving another alternative or a new combination of alternatives that increases the utility of settlement to the parties without decreasing their total payoffs.

When a final demand is made, the client worries whether to accept the lawyer's recommendation to settle or to go to trial. The lawyer should help the client understand how cases are processed through the legal system, the importance of trial as a standard of fairness and a forum for vindication of wrongs, and the tradeoffs involved in accepting what is certain over that which is uncertain.

In the emergence and crisis stage, negotiators using an integrative or problem-solving approach work toward closure. They trade concessions and find solutions that "bridge" the parties' needs and satisfy underlying interests.

4. STAGE FOUR: AGREEMENT OR FINAL BREAKDOWN

Stage Four involves two divergent paths. Either (1) the parties reach agreement, proceed to work out the details, and finalize the agreement or (2) the parties reach an impasse, negotiations break down, and the case goes to trial or the transaction is not consummated.

5. INTERPLAY BETWEEN THE LITIGATION PROCESS AND THE STAGES OF NEGOTIATION

Professor Williams aptly points out that the negotiation process operates concurrently with a competing process having a force and dynamic of its own: litigation. In the preceding discussion, the pressures for settlement were occasioned by trial deadlines. In reality, however, the arrival of the trial date is the culmination of a complex series of preparatory actions that begins before the case is filed. It proceeds step by step through the complex procedures of choosing a forum, pleading, discovery, preparation of witnesses, preparation of evidence (documentary and demonstrative), pretrial conference, motions, and all related work.

These aspects of legal procedure are undertaken (or have the potential of being undertaken) by the lawyers concurrently as the case moves, psychologically, through stages one to four of the negotiation process. Some procedures, such as pleading, coincide with basic elements of the negotiation process, such as statement of (extreme) opening positions. The utilization and timing of other procedural steps is a matter open to the discretion of the lawyers and can be used either to help or to hinder the psychology and dynamics of each successive stage in the negotiation process.

Professor Williams points out that effective negotiators will take full cognizance of the relationship between pretrial procedures and the stages in the negotiation process. Lawyers taking an adversarial approach will calculate their moves within the legal sphere to further their objectives of arriving, if possible, at a settlement more favorable than trial would produce. In a contract dispute between two reputable businesses, for example, it is commonly feasible and desirable to engage in the bargaining process and arrive at a suitable agreement without ever filing an action. Other alternative forms of dispute resolution, such as mediation and arbitration, may be considered. On the other hand, if one or both parties refuse to negotiate seriously, and other efforts or alternative means fail, a forum is selected and complaint filed. In a business context, this step is a serious one, and it may well be enough to produce serious attempts to resolve the case without trial. If not, then further pretrial procedures are undertaken step by step, frequently in ways that have the greatest strategic value for an advantageous settlement as well as maximum value in the event of trial.

This example illustrates the essential tension that exists between negotiation and formal legal processes. The former generally involves much less tension and the latter invokes the adversarial zero-sum approach of the formal legal system. The importance of restrained, conciliatory approaches to dispute resolution in the business context is often overlooked by lawyers who become accustomed to using the legal process as a means of putting direct and unmistakable pressure to bear on the opposing side. They come to accept this level of tension as normal and desirable. While this attitude may be appropriate in some kinds of cases, it is likely to diminish creative and mutually beneficial solutions that meet the parties' interests and needs in better ways.

CHAPTER 3

PLANNING, PREPARATION, AND WORKING WITH THE CLIENT

A. INTRODUCTION

As previously discussed, thorough preparation is one of the fundamental characteristics of effective legal negotiators. Much of this preparation involves working with the client. This chapter focuses on how to plan and prepare for legal negotiations, including understanding the proposed deal or transaction; determining the applicable law; assessing needs and interests of the parties; assessing strengths and weakness; investigating objective criteria; determining alternatives and options; developing realistic expectations; setting goals; and obtaining authority. This chapter also focuses on the critical skill of case evaluation as well as the process of drafting proposed agreements prior to negotiations.

B. UNDERSTANDING THE PROPOSED DEAL OR TRANSACTION

If you are representing a client in a transactional situation, an essential part of your preparation is understanding the proposed transaction. In their book, *Lawyers as Counselors: A Client-Centered*

Approach, Binder, Bergman, Price, and Tremblay suggest several steps in this regard.

1. OBTAINING DETAILED INFORMATION

Binder, Bergman, Price, and Tremblay suggest that the first level of inquiry and discussion with the client should focus on obtaining detailed information in the following categories:

(1) the terms and history of the proposed transaction;

(2) the timetable for finalizing the transaction;

(3) the client's objectives;

(4) the other party or parties;

(5) the client's business operations;

(6) how the transaction or business arrangement will function; and

(7) the economics of the transaction.

2. "DEAL SPECIFIC" MATTERS

The second level of inquiry and discussion suggested by Binder, Bergman, Price, and Tremblay is "deal-specific" matters, primarily the provisions covering important obligations ("operative" provisions) and risks ("contingent" or "remedial" provisions). This inquiry and discussion should seek to identify the client's goals and interests and how various alternative approaches could accomplish those goals or satisfy those interests.

Thus, a negotiator should learn from the client and other sources as much as possible about the business context in which the transaction is to take place ("industry knowledge"). What are the products or services to be bought, sold, or exchanged? What business practices or customs are relevant to the transaction? What timing concerns are relevant? What is the relationship of the parties? What are the standard terms in the industry for this type of agreement? Who are the key persons involved in carrying out the transaction? What economic and social interests affect the transaction? Will the terms of this transaction have potential effects on other transactions?

A negotiator should carefully determine what, if any, preliminary discussions have taken place between the parties and what remains open for negotiation. Likewise, it is useful to check if any public statements have been made by any of the parties. It may turn out that prior discussions between the parties have settled—or appear to have settled—many elements of the transaction (without the benefit of legal advice). A negotiator should also examine all documents relating to the discussion of the transaction prepared by the parties. It may turn out that a legally binding and enforceable agreement has already been reached. Are there points that need to be renegotiated? Binder, Bergman, Price, and Tremblay warn that it is important to learn precisely the terms of the parties' agreement because a draft agreement containing a different understanding might alienate the other side by causing it to think that the draft unilaterally changes the prior agreement.

3. DETERMINING THE APPLICABLE LAW

As part of the preparation for a transaction negotiation, a negotiator should determine the law applicable to the transaction—including relevant state or federal statutes, regulations, and judicial decisions. Does the Uniform Commercial Code govern the transaction? Do reporting requirements apply to the transaction, such as a pre-merger notification requirement? What are the standard form agreements, if any, for this type of transaction and how do they relate to the applicable law?

In this context, a negotiator should consider whether the negotiator would want to bargain for a "choice-of-law clause" making the law of a particular jurisdiction applicable to the transaction (*e.g.*, "This agreement shall be governed by, and construed in accordance with, the law of [jurisdiction]"). Such a clause may be particularly useful if the law varies substantially among the possible jurisdictions that might otherwise apply to the transaction.

Similarly, if a possible future dispute over the transaction is likely or possible, a negotiator should also consider negotiating for a "forum selection provision" or "dispute resolution clause." A forum selection provision regulates the location of suit (*e.g.*, "The parties agree that only the courts of [a particular forum] shall have jurisdiction over this contract and any disputes arising out of this contract.")

A "dispute resolution clause" provides the method for resolving future disputes. For example, a negotiator may want to consider negotiating for a clause providing for mediation, particularly when the parties to the transaction are going to have a continuing relationship because that process tends to resolve disputes in a manner that does not undermine the "mutual respect" between the parties.

Very comprehensive dispute resolution clauses are possible. For example, such a clause might require the parties to first "meet and confer" in an attempt to resolve a dispute. If that fails to resolve the dispute, then the parties might be required to participate in mediation. If that fails to resolve the dispute, then the parties might be required to submit the dispute to arbitration.

C. ASSESSING NEEDS AND INTERESTS OF THE PARTIES

After a proposed deal or transaction is understood, another important aspect of preparing to negotiate is to focus specifically on what the needs and interests of all the parties are and how they interact. The same process is also useful when the parties are involved in a dispute. Working with basic ideas developed by Fisher and Ury's "Circle Chart" and other planning suggestions, Bastress and Harbaugh in their book, *Interviewing, Counseling, and Negotiation*, have developed the following four steps to inventory, classify, compare, and satisfy the needs of the parties.

1. INVENTORY OF NEEDS, INTERESTS, AND OBJECTIVES OF THE PARTIES

The first step, an inventory, involves the extensive kind of review and analysis that was suggested in Chapter 2(D), above. Bastress and Harbaugh recommend that the lawyer and the client independently prepare lists of needs and interests. Then working together, the lawyer and client develop a single list, along with descriptive phrases that capture the essence of those needs, interests, and objectives.

2. CLASSIFYING THE PARTIES' NEEDS AND INTERESTS

The second step is to classify the parties' needs and interests. Bastress and Harbaugh suggest using three categories: (1) "absolutely essential" ("true deal-breakers"); (2) "important" (high priority "but probably will not force a deadlock if they cannot be met in the exact form they are sought"); and (3) "desirable." They warn against the tendency to place every need and interest in the "absolutely essential" category. For purposes of beginning to classify the needs and interests of the parties, they also suggest that it is easiest to start with those of the lawyer's own client.

In the course of identifying the parties' needs and objectives and preparing for negotiation, a legal negotiator should focus on what weight or value *each party* gives to each of the variety of interests. In particular, lawyers should be careful not to substitute their own calculus of what solution or negotiating

stance to adopt for that of their clients. Valuing
nonlegal concerns especially falls within the client's
domain. Binder, Bergman, Price, and Tremblay point
out that nonlegal concerns often outweigh legal ones.
Even desired solutions ordinarily entail negative
nonlegal consequences.

Furthermore, by opting for the positive nonlegal
consequences of one choice, a client may have to forgo
positive nonlegal consequences of alternative options.
Thus, a client may have to balance goals in light of a
variety of factors or choose between solutions that
require the client to trade one set of negative consequences for another. Allowing the client to make
these decisions and to set priorities on the interests
and concerns will provide greater client satisfaction.
It will also provide better guidance to how the legal
negotiator can best serve the client's interests and
achieve the client's objectives in a legal negotiation.

3. COMPARISON OF THE PARTIES' NEEDS AND INTERESTS

The third step involves a comparison of the parties'
needs and interests. To accomplish this comparison,
Bastress and Harbaugh recommend the use of three
categories: (1) "shared" needs or interests (common
goals); (2) "independent" needs or interests of each
party (unrelated concerns); and (3) "conflicting" needs
and interests. They suggest using the following chart,
reproduced with permission (in reduced size), to "help
visualize, refine, and understand the underlying
needs and interests of the parties."

	SHARED NEEDS	INDEPENDENT NEEDS		CONFLICTING NEEDS	
		Party #1	Party #2	Party #1	Party #2
ESSENTIAL					
IMPORTANT					
DESIRABLE					

4. SEARCH FOR SOLUTIONS

The fourth step suggested by Bastress and Harbaugh involves a search for solutions. Fisher and Ury suggest that the key to developing solutions or creating options is first to invent them and then to evaluate them. One way to invent solutions or options is brainstorming—*first* listing all of them and *then* evaluating them. The evaluation process may stimulate additional options. Similarly, by identifying the rationale or theory behind each option and then searching for other options that would achieve the same result, new options may be invented.

In *Getting to Yes: Negotiating Agreement Without Giving In*, Fisher and Ury also suggest that options may be invented by looking through the eyes of experts—for example, how would other professionals or specialists in various fields approach the problem and resolve it. Furthermore, in the course of a negotiation, it may be useful to divide the problem into smaller units or segments, reserving some issues for later and thinking of temporary solutions. In other words, as Fisher and Ury state, "change the scope of the problem." In this way, the negotiators may gain a new perspective and again stimulate options.

D. ASSESSING STRENGTHS AND WEAKNESSES AND IMPROVING NEGOTIATING POWER

As previously discussed, effective legal negotiators are described as being "analytical," "realistic," "rational," and "reasonable." An important aspect of having such characteristics is paying close attention to the *relative strengths* and *weaknesses* of the parties.

1. RELATIVE POWER AND LEVERAGE

Strengths and weakness are a reflection of *power and leverage—"the ability of a negotiator to influence the behavior of an opponent."* In thinking about power during the preparation process, one needs to be careful not to misinterpret the relative power of the parties by overemphasizing one factor and failing to keep the negotiating situation in perspective.

For example, in *Getting to Yes: Negotiating Agreement Without Giving In*, Fisher and Ury illustrate this point in relation to wealth. One would normally think that a wealthy person would be "powerful" when negotiating with a poor person. However, consider Fisher and Ury's wealthy tourist who wants to buy a small brass pot for a modest price from a vendor at the Bombay railroad station. The seller may be poor, but the seller is likely to know the market. If the vendor does not sell the pot to this tourist, the vendor can sell it to another. Based on experience, the seller can estimate when and for how much the pot could be sold to someone else. In this situation, the wealthy tourist will, in fact, be weak unless the tourist knows approximately how much it would cost and how difficult it would be to find a comparable pot elsewhere.

According to Fisher and Ury, it is almost certain that the tourist will either miss the chance to buy such a pot or will pay too high a price. Thus, the tourist's wealth in no way strengthens the tourist's negotiating power. Furthermore, if the tourist's wealth is apparent, it weakens the tourist's ability to buy the pot at a low price. As Fisher and Ury aptly observe, to convert the tourist's wealth into negotiating power, the tourist would have to apply it to learn about the price at which the tourist could buy an equally or more attractive brass pot somewhere else.

In *The Negotiating Game*, Chester L. Karrass identifies eight "basic principles of power" to be kept in mind when power is being assessed: (1) "power is always relative" because a party's power is seldom absolute; (2) "power may be real or apparent" because the influence of power depends on the perception of the parties—*i.e.*, an advantage or disadvantage means nothing if the parties fail to perceive it; (3) "power may be exerted without action" when "the opponent *believes* that action can and will be taken"; (4) "power is always limited" and "its range depends upon the situation, government regulations, ethical standards, and present or future competition"; (5) "power exists to the extent that it is accepted"; as Karrass points out, some parties "are simply less willing to be dominated than others and would rather do without than be exploited"; (6) "the ends of power cannot be separated from the means"; thus, for example, "[o]ne cannot hope to develop a loyal customer by using exploitive tactics"; (7) "the exercise of power always entails cost and risk"; and (8) "power relationships change over time."

In *Smart Negotiating: How to Make Good Deals in the Real World*, James C. Freund suggests that leverage can be visualized in terms of a "playing field." Freund notes that the playing field in a negotiation is often not "level." One party usually wants the agreement more than the other or one party is participating in the negotiation "less voluntarily" than the other. Thus, "[w]hen the playing field is unlevel for whatever reason, it creates leverage."

According to Freund, the four most common "leverage" factors affecting the "level of the playing field" are (1) "necessity"; (2) "desire"; (3) "competition"; and (4) "time." Each of these factors, along with others, should be carefully assessed with the assistance of the client and other sources of information as part of thorough preparation for a negotiation.

First, is *necessity* pushing one of the parties into the transaction? Necessity creates negative leverage that can be exploited. For example, a seller may be forced into the transaction because the seller must immediately raise cash. This extreme pressure may result in the seller being willing to accept less than the seller could have received had the seller been able to delay the sale and find additional potential buyers.

Second, is strong *desire* motivating one of the parties? As Fruend aptly points out, the critical question is, "[w]ho *wants* the deal more, and how strongly does he or she feel about it?" Such disparity "creates a real advantage for the cooler party, the one who's more willing to risk losing the deal."

Third, is there *competition* (*i.e.*, multiple potential buyers or sellers)? For example, in a potential sale transaction, the presence of multiple bidders tends to force the successful bidder to pay "top dollar, while stiffening the seller's resolve to hold out for it."

Fourth, is one of the parties under *time* pressure or forced to meet a deadline? As Freund points out, "[a] party acting under a deadline that has no impact on the other side often makes decisions and takes actions that vary from what his or her conduct might be under more relaxed circumstances. Unfortunately, these decisions and action have a way of playing right into the other party's hands."

2. IMPROVING NEGOTIATING POWER THROUGH PREPARATION

a. *Researching and Improving Alternatives*

One way of improving a party's negotiating power is to have one or more alternative ways of satisfying the party's needs. If a negotiator enters into a negotiation without knowing the client's best alternative to a negotiated agreement ("BATNA") (discussed in Chapter 2), the negotiator's power is weakened. On the other hand, when a negotiator's preparation has made the client's alternatives clear and certain, the negotiator can readily test the attractiveness of the other side's settlement offers by comparing them with the client's alternatives. As Fisher and Ury point out, the better the alternative, the easier it will be to walk away.

b. *Researching Ways to Provide What the Other Side Is Likely to Want*

The search for solutions and options described in the preceding section may provide ways of providing what the other side is likely to want or need. Being able to meet those wants and needs creates "positive leverage."

c. *Considering the Other Side's Potential Losses*

Psychologists have found that potential losses "loom larger" in a negotiating party's mind than do equivalent gains. As part of preparing for a negotiation, it is important to research whether some kind of potential loss could be imposed on the other side if a mutually satisfactory agreement is not reached.

For example, assume that a buyer wants to obtain a patented or temporarily scarce item from a seller. The scarceness of the item may tempt the seller to

negotiate for a high price for the item. However, a
seller would probably think twice about doing so if the
buyer purchased several other product lines that are
highly competitive from the seller. If the buyer makes
it known that all of the buyer's business could go
elsewhere, the potential loss of that business is likely
to be a greater concern than perhaps the equivalent
high profit on the scarce item.

d. Researching Objective Standards

In *Getting to Yes: Negotiating Agreement Without
Giving In*, Fisher and Ury assert that objective
criteria or standards provide a much better means of
reconciling directly conflicting interests than a
"contest of wills." They maintain that no negotiation
will be efficient or really amicable if, as in positional
bargaining, each side pits its will against the other's.
As Fischer and Ury point out, one side will have to
"back down." The difference between a contest of wills
and objective criteria or standards is encapsulated in
the following two questions: "How much are you
willing to pay for this product or to settle this case?"
versus "What is this product or case worth?"

Objective criteria and standards exist independent
of will. They exist for almost every aspect of a
negotiation. These criteria and standards include the
following:

- current market price
- comparable sales transactions
- precedent
- laws, rules, and regulations

- what a court or agency would decide
- professional standards
- efficiency
- moral standards
- expert or third-party opinion
- scientific judgment
- tradition
- reciprocity
- industry standards
- costs
- equal treatment
- trade custom
- prior comparable jury verdicts
- design and safety standards

To demonstrate how objective standards would influence a negotiation, assume that the "value" of real property is at issue. One party may "believe" that the property is worth $200,000, and the other party may "feel" that the property is only worth $100,000. In contrast to those beliefs and feelings, an objective standard would be the value of similar properties based on recent comparable sales.

Furthermore, strength can be gained by framing proposals within the other party's likely interests and objective standards that they are likely to accept as "legitimate" ones.

3. PLANNING QUESTIONS TO ASK

Researchers have found that negotiators can use questions effectively for various purposes. First, they can be used to gain attention—for example, "How are you doing today?" Second, they can be used to obtain information. For example, a negotiator might ask, "What does your client want to get from this negotiation?" or "What are your client's damages?" Third, questions can be used to provide information. For example, a negotiator might ask, "Do you know that this type of evidence cannot be presented to the jury?" or "Do you know that my client will be out of work for six more weeks?" Fourth, they can be used to stimulate thinking. For example, a negotiator might ask, "Have you ever considered the possibility that my client might decide to buy the product elsewhere?" ("Why" and "how" questions are also typically used for this purpose.) Fifth, they can be used to bring the discussion to a conclusion. For example, a negotiator might ask, "Do we have an agreement then?"

In preparing for a negotiation, a negotiator could devise a series of questions following the above patterns to cover the entire negotiation. Thus, a negotiator could plan to ask attention-getting questions at the start of the negotiation, followed by questions obtaining information. Both open-ended and closed questions could be used. Then, a negotiator could plan to stimulate the opposing negotiator's thinking by questioning. Finally, a negotiator could ask questions that bring the discussion to a conclusion. In this way, the negotiator can force the opposing side to do most of the talking and still control the direction of the negotiation.

The value of asking questions during a negotiation should not be underestimated. For example, when a negotiator states a demand ("My client will not accept less than $100,000 in settlement") or sets a deadline ("The goods must be delivered by the end of next month"), asking for the reasons will often reveal critical information. A negotiator will likely find something in the answer that can be discussed— rather than the demand or deadline itself. It may also lead to possibilities for integrative bargaining or creative problem solving. The answer may also expose erroneous assumptions or information, or it may give the negotiator a sound basis for rejecting the demand. Likewise, by making two proposals at once or by using a series of hypotheticals and asking the other side which proposal or hypothetical is preferable, important information can sometimes be gained.

Commentators point out that some kinds of questions tend to cause trouble. For example, avoid questions that offend or condemn. Likewise, avoid questions that polarize the discussion, such as, "What do you think of this proposal?" Avoid leading questions. Avoid questions that attempt to force others into your point of view, either by reflecting what you have said or incorporating your preconceived view. Also, avoid impulse questions. In any event, explaining the reason for asking a question helps avoid some of these problems. For example, a question that seeks information could be introduced by raising a personal need, "Could we take a moment to clear up something for me?"

Several widely recognized techniques can be used to avoid answering the opposing negotiator's questions. These "blocking techniques" are discussed in the next chapter.

E. CASE EVALUATION

A specialized aspect of assessing a party's strengths and weaknesses in a legal dispute is "the value of a case." As discussed in Chapter 2, legal disputes are often negotiated "in the shadow of the law." In the past, legal education centered on the adversary system as the principal dispute-resolution model for lawyers. The adversary approach to legal disputes assumes that the task of lawyers is to present the facts and the law in their strategically most favorable light to a judge or jury, who will determine what is the truth and will award dollar damages commensurate with the wrong. This conception of valuation shifts the ultimate responsibility for calculating damages to judge or jury. Furthermore, it induces lawyers to think of case value primarily in terms of probable jury verdicts—and not in other ways.

The results of experimental negotiations and empirical studies vividly demonstrate that dramatic differences can exist in the perceptions of the value of a case. For instance, one lawyer may regard a given situation as a $50,000 case, but others may *genuinely* see it as a $15,000, $30,000, $60,000, or $90,000 case. Indeed, a group of typical lawyers may easily vary by one hundred percent or more in placing a predicted value on complex cases. Thus, a critical point to remember is that case value is a *range*, not one fixed amount.

During the negotiation process, each side's expectations about what can be obtained in the case can undergo substantial changes. One of the principal tasks of effective negotiators is to convince opponents of a possible range of trial outcomes (case value) and of a real risk that the outcome may be as high (or as low) as they suggest. In this regard, another critical point to remember is that one negotiator can influence another negotiator's view of case value through initial positioning and negotiation conduct.

1. BASIC ELEMENTS OF CASE VALUE

Lawyers' perceptions of case value are an amalgamation of various factors, legal rules, uncertainties, and predictions.

a. *Certainty of Liability*

One factor that must be taken into account in valuing a case is the certainty of liability (the legal obligation to pay). In some cases, liability will be conceded or not seriously contested. In most cases, however, liability may be vigorously contested on either factual or legal grounds—or both. As part of effective preparation, negotiators must find ways to deal with substantive weaknesses and to present legal and factual matters in the most favorable light.

Legally, the dispute may center on the applicable law, existence of the legal theory or defense in the jurisdiction, burden of proof, or procedural legal issues. Often, those issues may not be fully resolved without an appeal. Factually, the dispute may center on simple facts (*e.g.*, Did the defendant stop at the stop sign?) or on more complex scientific, economic, or technical issues. Many factual ambiguities can finally be resolved only by submitting the dispute to an independent trier of fact, such as a court or arbitrator. In such cases, the relative skills and diligence in fact gathering of investigators and lawyers on both sides will often determine the outcome.

b. Elements and Measure of Damages

In addition to taking into account the certainty of liability, lawyers must carefully consider the elements and measures of damages in making case evaluations. From the plaintiff's point of view, for purposes of negotiation and trial preparation, the tasks of a lawyer are to (1) identify the remedies potentially available, (2) select the one or ones that will best serve the client's needs, (3) find authority to support the facts of the case, and (4) support a measurement of the remedy or remedies that is the most generous to the plaintiff.

i. Judicial Remedies

The principal judicial remedy is the awarding of damages. This remedy concentrates on compensation —making good the plaintiff's losses—measured in some way, such as the diminished value, cost of repair, or replacement cost. Some elements of the damage remedy, however, are not entirely compensatory, such as punitive damages. In contrast, restitutionary remedies are normally given to prevent unjust enrichment of the defendant and are measured by the defendant's gains. For example, restitution is used to recover a wrongdoer's profits. It is also a common form of remedy when rescission or reformation of a contract takes place.

Another important category of judicial remedies includes coercive remedies, such as a decree for specific performance or injunctive relief. These coercive remedies are backed by the court's contempt power. A related form of relief is a declaratory judgment setting out the rights of the parties or construing an instrument.

ii. General Damages

Courts have developed rules of damage recovery based on general models of expected loss. These rules (formulas) are known as general damages. Each kind of legal injury has its own general-damages rule. Thus, there is a general-damages rule for breach of a land contract, for negligently inflicted personal injuries, trespass to land, etc. Primarily for administrative convenience, courts are willing to assume this general-damages measure of loss without requiring any subjective showing of real loss. For example, a plaintiff sometimes may not be actually worse off because of the trespass or contract breach, yet the plaintiff is allowed damages under the general-damages formula.

General-damages rules usually provide for measurement in terms of value. For example, in eminent domain (condemnation) cases, the landowner is awarded the market value for the land, considering the highest and best use for which the land is reasonably adapted. Similarly, when tangible property is destroyed, the general-damages measure is the market value of the chattel at the time and place of destruction (with adjustments for salvage value). When tangible property is damaged but not destroyed, the traditional general-damages measure is the difference between the value of the chattel immediately before and the value immediately after the damage (depreciation in value). Not all courts, however, follow the same general-damages rules. For example, some courts allow the reasonable cost of restoring damaged but not destroyed property to substantially its pre-damage condition (cost of repair).

iii. Special Damages

In addition to general damages, plaintiffs may sometimes recover "special damages," which are more or less peculiar to a particular plaintiff and would not be expected to occur regularly to other plaintiffs in similar circumstances. For example, the general-damages recovery for converted property is the value of the chattel at time and place of conversion (usually with interest from that time). If the plaintiff reasonably incurs expense pursuing the converted property, that expense is recoverable as special damages. Other items of special damages that have been allowed in this situation include the owner's cost of a replevin bond posted to recover immediate possession of the converted property and rewards paid to induce third persons to aid in locating the converted property.

Courts place three important limitations on special damages, making their recovery more difficult. First, special damages must have been caused in fact by the defendant's actionable conduct. Thus, if the special damages would have occurred in the absence of the defendant's tort or breach of contract, the plaintiff ordinarily would not be permitted to recover. Second, special damages must be proved with reasonable certainty. This restriction often prevents recovery of lost profits. Third, special damages must not be deemed too remote. In tort cases, special damages are often refused under the "proximate cause" restriction —the defendant's tort did not proximately cause them. In contract cases, this type of "remote" damage is often denied on the ground that it was not "within the contemplation of the parties at the time of contracting" or that it was not "foreseeable."

c. *Timing of Payments*

In terms of evaluating the value of a settlement from the plaintiff's perspective, dollars paid today are generally better than dollars paid a year from today. The value of future dollars may be eroded by inflation, and dollars paid today may be put to use immediately (*e.g.*, earning interest or invested in the plaintiff's business). Furthermore, uncertain future conditions create the possibility that the dollars may never be paid by the defendant (*e.g.*, the defendant may file for bankruptcy and pay only cents on the dollar of the settlement obligation). From the defendant's perspective, the opposite is generally true. Paying future dollars may be less costly because of inflation, and the defendant can ordinarily retain interest earned prior to a judgment on unliquidated amounts.

i. Calculating the Present or Future Value of Any One Future Payment or Receipt

When dollars are paid today to cover expected pecuniary losses or other amounts that would be received in the *future*, a reduction to "present value" may be legally necessary. Assume, for example, that the plaintiff would have received a bonus of $500,000, five years from now, under a contract. Assume further that the contract has been breached and that the defendant is liable for the $500,000 payment. If a court awarded a lump sum of $500,000 today to compensate the plaintiff for loss of that bonus, in the view of most courts the plaintiff would be "overcompensated" because the plaintiff would be able to earn interest presently on money that otherwise would have been unavailable for five years.

In contrast, some jurisdictions, particularly when supported by expert testimony, have allowed a "total offset" approach, which assumes the inflation rate and discount rate cancel each other out, so there is no reduction for discount and no increase for inflation.

To adjust this future value (*FV* in the formula below) to its present value (*PV* in the formula below), you must make three determinations. First, you must know or determine what the total future value will be.

In this instance, it is set by the contract at $500,000. Second, you must determine the number of periods (n in the formula below) that interest will be paid. This determination is necessary to take into account the compounding effect of paying the interest (annually or quarterly, for example). Thus, for the example given above, n might be 5 or 20 (based on 5 annual periods (5 x 1) or 20 quarterly periods (5 x 4). Assume that the interest will be paid and compounded quarterly for this example ($n = 20$).

Third, you must determine the interest rate per period (i in the formula below) that will be paid on the present sum. The plaintiff will want the court to use a low interest rate; the defendant will want the court to use a high rate. In terms of result, the rate is a critical factor. For purposes of this example, assume that the interest rate will be eight percent. This annual rate, however, must be converted into the rate per period—in this instance, 2% (8 divided by 4).

These figures could then be used in the following formula to determine the present value of the $500,000 bonus:

$$PV = FV \left[\frac{1}{(1+i)} \right]^n$$

Substituting the known items in this formula ($500,000 for FV, .02 for i, and 20 for n) yields a present value (PV) of $336,486. This adjustment is called *discounting* the amount.

The above calculation can also easily be made using a hand-held financial calculator that has specific keys for entering each of the known values. Present value tables are also available for this purpose. Shown below is an excerpt from such a table:

PRESENT VALUE OF $1

Period	1%	**2%**	3%	4%	5%	6%	...
1	.9901	.9804	.9709	.9615	.9524	.9434	...
2	.9803	.9612	.9426	.9246	.9070	.8900	...
...	...	...	...	...	...	...	...
20	.8195	**.6730**	.5537	.4564	.3769	.3118	...

To use this table to calculate the present value of the bonus, you would find the row covering twenty periods on the vertical axis. The figure for two percent is .6730. Thus, to calculate the present value of the $500,000 bonus, you simply multiply $500,000 times .6730, which equals $336,500. As you can see, use of a table or a formula may produce slight differences ($336,500 versus $336,486 above).

Sometimes, you will need to determine the future value of a present payment or offer. This adjustment is called *compounding* the amount. For example, assume that the defendant offers to pay $25,000 for purposes of settling a $60,000 payment due ten years from now. Is this a good offer? At this point, you do not know the interest rate the defendant used nor the number of periods for which interest will be paid. In deciding whether this offer is a good one from the plaintiff's perspective, you should consider what rate reflects the value of money to your client (which may be significantly different than the value to the defendant). Assume, for instance, your client has the opportunity to safely invest the money for a ten-year term at twelve percent rate compounded quarterly.

To calculate the future value (*FV* in the formula below) to your client of the present offer ($25,000) (*PV* in the formula below) under these circumstances, you would insert a three percent interest rate per period (12 divided by 4) (*i* in the formula below) for the correct number of periods (*n* in the formula below, with *n* equal to 40—10 x 4) as follows:

$$FV = PV (1 + i)^n \text{ or } FV = \$25,000 (1 + .03)^{40}$$

In this instance, the future value of the offer under the conditions noted is $81,551. Thus, the offer would be a favorable one from your client's perspective.

Again, a table can be used to determine the future value of an amount of money at the end of a given number of periods, as shown in the excerpt below:

FUTURE VALUE OF $1 AT THE END OF n PERIODS

Period	1%	2%	**3%**	...
1	1.0100	1.0200	1.0300	...
2	1.0201	1.0404	1.0609	...
...	...	...	...	...
40	1.4889	2.2080	**3.2620**	...

Using the above table to make the calculation, the future value of the $25,000 offer under the assumed conditions is $81,550 ($25,000 x 3.2620).

ii. Calculating the Present Value of a Stream of Future Payments or Receipts

Assume that you represent a totally and permanently disabled client who was injured as a result of the defendant's negligence. Assume also that your client is legally entitled to recover for lost earning capacity (money that your client could have earned, but now cannot earn, in the future). One way to compensate your client would be to have the defendant make the weekly or monthly payments as they accrue. Apart from workers' compensation acts or other statutory authorization, such as the Model Periodic Payments of Judgment Act, however, courts ordinarily award lump sums, not periodic installment payments.

To avoid "overcompensating" the plaintiff (for the reasons discussed in the preceding subsections), most jurisdictions allow the defendant to request that the lump sum of the total future earnings be reduced to its present value. The sum should be the present value of the future stream of payments (an annuity) so that neither the amount awarded nor interest on it remains at the end of the loss period.

To calculate this sum (*PVA* = present value of an annuity in the formula below), three things must be determined. First, the interest rate per period must be set (*i* = interest per period in the formula below). Courts have taken varying approaches in setting that rate. For example, some provide a fixed figure, such as four percent, compounded quarterly. Others rely on the "common sense" of the jury to select the rate. Assume that a six percent annual rate would be used.

Second, the length of time (stated in terms of the correct number of periods) that the plaintiff would have received that income must be determined. That evidence would most likely be provided by using a mortality table (which attempts to show a person's normal life expectancy). Assume that the plaintiff has a normal life expectancy of fifteen additional years. Because the interest will be compounded annually, the total number of periods (n in the formula below) would be 15 (15 x 1). If the interest would have been compounded quarterly, this figure would be 60 (15 x 4) and the rate per period would be 1.5% (6 divided by 4).

Third, the fixed payment per period must be determined. For example, assume that you have evidence to show that your client would have had an annual earning capacity of $40,000 ($p$ = fixed payment per period in the formula below). If the period had been quarterly, the fixed payment per period would be $10,000 ($40,000 divided by 4).

Thus, to determine the present value of an ordinary or regular (deferred) annuity (in which the payment is made at the end of each period) based upon the above example, the following values would be inserted in this formula (p = $40,000, i = 6%, n = 15 years):

$$PVA = p \left[\frac{1 - \frac{1}{(1+i)^n}}{i} \right]$$

Entering these known values into a financial calculator to solve this formula, the present value of the annuity would be $388,490. To determine the value of an annuity due (in which the payment is made at the beginning of each period rather than the end), you would press a [DUE] key on most calculators to modify the calculation appropriately. In this instance, the present value would change to $411,799 to fund an annuity due.

Tables are also available for this purpose ("Present Value of an Annuity of $1 Per Period for *n* Periods"). By using the known interest rate (6%) and the number of payments (15), you can determine a factor by which the fixed payment ($40,000) can be multiplied. As indicated in the following table, that factor is 9.7122.

PRESENT VALUE OF AN ANNUITY OF $1 PER PERIOD FOR *n* PERIODS

Number of Payments	1%	2%	...	**6%**	...
1	0.9901	0.9804	...	0.9434	...
2	1.9704	1.9416	...	1.8334	...
...	...	...	...	...	...
15	13.8651	12.8493	...	**9.7122**	...

Multiplying $40,000 times 9.7122 yields a present value of $388,488 for an ordinary or regular annuity.

d. Taxation

Another basic element of case value is taxation. Indeed, the value of a recovery or settlement may be enhanced (or reduced) considerably depending on its tax treatment. With respect to taxation, the interests of the parties are often at odds on tax issues. Most of the tax rules are structured to give favorable tax treatment at one end of the transaction or the other, but not at both. Nonetheless, tax treatment may create the opportunity to add significant value to a settlement. Generally speaking, the tax treatment depends upon two primary factors: (1) the characterization of the values exchanged for tax purposes, and (2) the timing of the payments.

i. Plaintiffs

For the plaintiff, the basic tax question is whether the money received will be taxed and, if so, when and at what rate? Except for amounts taken as a medical deduction in a prior year, § 104(a)(2) of the Internal Revenue Code excludes from a plaintiff's gross income "the amount of any damages other than punitive damages received (whether by suit or agreement and whether as lump sums or periodic payments) on account of personal physical injuries or physical sickness."

This favorable tax treatment of personal injury recoveries or settlements in large measure accounts for the rapid growth of "structured settlements" in personal injury cases (discussed in the next section and in later chapters). If the plaintiff received a lump sum and then invested it, the interest earned would be taxable. On the other hand, if the plaintiff receives a structured settlement—a series of varying periodic or balloon payments from the defendant on account of personal injuries or death—these payments are entirely excludable from the plaintiff's gross income. The Periodic Payment Settlement Act of 1982, amending 26 U.S.C.A. § 104, codified prior IRS rulings and specifically authorized this exclusion.

In contrast to the favorable tax treatment given to personal injury recoveries and settlements, an amount received by means of a judgment or settlement that represents damages for loss of profits in a business is ordinarily includable in the plaintiff's gross income. Likewise, an amount awarded as punitive damages is normally includable in gross income as ordinary income. For example, in the leading case of *Commissioner v. Glenshaw Glass Co.* (1955), the punitive portions of a settlement in an antitrust and fraud case was held to be includable in gross income.

ii. Defendants

With regard to defendants, a large savings will result if the settlement payment is deductible from the defendant's gross income rather than payable with after-tax dollars. The after-tax cost to the defendant also depends on the timing of an allowable deduction. If the payment is deductible, can it all be deducted in this tax year, or must it be capitalized, so that the tax benefits are available, if at all, through amortization or depreciation over several years?

Specifically, amounts paid by defendants to satisfy judgments or to settle claims generally may be deducted only when those amounts are ordinary and necessary expenses for the carrying on of a trade or business. Defendants who are not carrying on a trade or business may be allowed to deduct expenses for production and collection of income or for management, conservation, or maintenance of property held for production and collection of income.

Defendants may not deduct payments relating to capital expenditures, acquisition of property, disposition of a capital asset, defenses of title, or recovery of property. Depreciation and amortization of such expenditures, however, may be deducted in certain situations as allowed by the Code.

e. *Effectiveness of Counsel*

In addition to certainty of liability, elements of damage, time-value of money, and taxation, another important element influencing case value—although not directly related to the merits—is the trial advocacy skill of the opposing lawyers. Because cases tend to be valued in terms of probable trial outcome, trial effectiveness either enhances or detracts from the credibility of statements and predictions made in negotiating sessions.

f. *Leverage*

As discussed in the preceding section, "leverage" is another factor influencing case value that is not directly related to the merits. In a litigation context, particular concerns or needs of the individual parties may enhance or decrease settlement value. For example, a party may be willing to pay a premium to settle rather than to face a possible clarification or change in the law that the case may entail. Similarly, one party may be particularly interested in avoiding adverse publicity for social, political, or business reasons.

g. *Insurance Coverage*

As a practical matter, the extent of insurance coverage may provide a limit on case value. Unless the insurer breaches its duty to settle within the policy limits when the plaintiff offers to settle the claim within the coverage of the insurance policy, it often matters little what the full amount of damages are. They are most likely uncollectible.

2. METHODS OF EVALUATION

Unfortunately, case evaluation techniques are generally not taught in most law schools nor has the bar developed more sophisticated methods of planning, research, financial analysis, and decision making that are routinely used in other professions to analyze value in a particular situation. Thus, the ability to make skilled estimates of case value has remained primarily an experience-based skill that focuses on the prediction of jury behavior.

a. Past Jury Verdicts in Similar Cases

Prediction of a probable trial outcome is an important basis for assigning a dollar or other value to a case. As part of this predictive process, lawyers may refer to published reports of jury verdicts to aid in case evaluation. These reports are useful not only for evaluating specific injuries, but also for evaluating the likelihood of finding liability.

i. Likelihood of a Favorable Verdict

Aids for predicting the likelihood of a favorable verdict include the "Liability Recovery Probabilities" volumes of the *Personal Injury Valuation Handbooks* published by LRP Publications. This type of service provides statistical information about cases by categories—intersection collisions, rear-end collisions, head-on collisions, change-of-lane collisions, railroad-crossing collisions, parking-lot collisions, plaintiff seated in rear of a parked car, etc. This series also has volumes presenting statistical studies of psychological factors—minors as plaintiffs, obesity, public utilities as defendants, injuries in taverns, questionable morals, joining of added defendant, participant sport accidents, and power mower accidents.

Information from these types of sources may provide insights in how a jury will react to particular situations. For example, despite what lawyers think, studies show that the highest rate of plaintiff recovery in accidents involving pedestrians occurs in cases in which a person is struck by a car while walking with traffic, on the side of a highway, during a period of limited visibility, possibly wearing dark clothing. In contrast, actual trial results show that a high proportion of cases involving a child so young as to be legally considered incapable of contributory negligence and thus entitled to a plaintiff's verdict result, in fact, in a defendant's verdict.

ii. Range of Damages

There are several aids for predicting the amount of damages. These include publications like the *Personal Injury Valuation Handbooks* (LRP Publications) and software programs used by the insurance industry. The published sources generally present ranges and expectancies. Some sources also present verdicts specifically deemed adequate, inadequate, or excessive. These sources are used by consulting the type of injury—back and neck strains, nose injuries, spinal cord injuries, hand injuries, etc.

b. Rules of Thumb

In evaluating routine personal injury cases, some lawyers and insurance claims adjusters have developed rules of thumb that produce a value based on some multiple of "special damages" or actual medical and other costs of the injury. Such rules of thumb may use an arbitrary multiplier as low as two or three or as high as ten. In cases involving more complex damages such as continued pain and suffering, evaluators sometimes use an arbitrary fixed dollar amount per week for general pain and suffering—for example, $200 per week of the period of total disability and $100 per week for the period of partial disability.

These rules of thumb may provide "ballpark" figures, but they obviously ignore individual differences between cases and severely simplify issues of actual harm done. The task of a plaintiff's lawyer is often to "leap over" these conventional rules of thumb. In other words, the plaintiff's lawyer must convince the opposing party of a real risk of a higher award that justifies a deviation from some arbitrary rule of thumb.

c. Formulas

Formulas provide another approach to evaluating case value. Formulas take into account a greater variety of factors than the simple rules of thumb do. In this way, lawyers attempt to arrive at a more sophisticated prediction of case value. This approach also helps lawyers consider each component systematically. Formulas are useful to the extent they help lawyers arrive at an objective valuation.

One widely recognized formula has been developed by Robert L. Simons. This formula subdivides the case into six categories and requires the lawyer to estimate a value for each. These categories are:

PAV—the probable average verdict;
PPV—the probability of a plaintiff's verdict;
UV—the uncollectible portion of the verdict;
PC—the plaintiff's cost in obtaining the verdict;
DC—the defendant's estimated cost of defense;
I—the value of intangible factors.

Expressed algebraically, the formula for the fair settlement value (FSV) is:

$(PAV \times PPV) - UV - PC + DC \pm I = FSV.$

Another widely recognized formula has been developed by Joseph and David Sindell. This formula uses a percentage point approach. To use this formula, up to a total of one hundred points is assigned based on the following six factors:

_____ *Liability* (1-50) (possible directed verdict; case will go to jury; doubtful, poor, fair, good, absolute, aggravated liability) (point value is listed lowest point value to highest—for example, a poor liability case might receive 20 points; a case with aggravated liability would receive 50 points)

_____ *Injuries* (1-10) (minor, mild, moderate, severe, conscious pain and suffering, death) (minor injuries might receive 2 points; death would receive 10 points)

_____ *Age of plaintiff* (1-10) (over 66 = 1 pt., 61-65 yrs. = 2 pts., 56-60 yrs. = 3 pts., 48-55 yrs. = 4 pts., 40-47 yrs. = 5 pts., 32-39 yrs. = 6 pts., 24-31 yrs. = 7 pts., 16-23 pts. = 8 pts., 8-15 yrs. = 9 pts., 1-7 yrs. = 10 pts.)

_____ *Type of plaintiff* (1-10) (refuses to go to court or dangerous, poor, fair, good, excellent) (10 points for an excellent plaintiff in terms of appearance, intelligence, and ability to withstand cross-examination)

_____ *Type of defendant(s)* (1-10) (jury may like, individual, jury may punish, affluent, target) (10 points for a target corporate defendant)

_____ *Out-of-pocket expense* (1-10) (1 point for every $100 up to 10 points ($1000); if the total out-of-pocket expense is over $1000, the overage ($_____) will be added below to determine the final settlement figure).

After these points have been totaled, the next step is to determine the most probable jury verdict obtainable in the case (based upon the verdict returned in similar cases in the jurisdiction where this case would be tried). This amount would be divided by 100 to determine the point value of the probable jury verdict:

Probable jury verdict ($_____) divided by 100 = $_____ Point Value of the Probable Jury Verdict).

To arrive at the final valuation, (1) multiply the point value of the probable jury verdict by the total point value of the case, and then (2) add the out-of-pocket expense over $1000:

$_____ (POINT VALUE OF PROBABLE JURY VERDICT) x _____ (TOTAL POINTS IN THIS CASE) = _____ + EXPENSE OVER $1000 $_____ = $ _____ FULL SETTLEMENT VALUE.

d. *Group Evaluation*

Another method of examining the value of a particular case is group evaluation. This method involves the review of the case by several persons to develop a collective judgment. Thus, a law firm may have an internal group of lay persons or lawyers provide their judgments of case value or other issues, such as the degree of the plaintiff's negligence in a comparative negligence case. This approach can be combined with staged, videotaped examinations of the plaintiff, defendant, and key witnesses (or substitutes playing them). Lawyers outside the firm can also be consulted.

e. *Professional Economic Analysis*

As noted earlier, structured settlements provide the plaintiff with favorable tax benefits. Structured settlements also have the advantage of tailoring the payments to the individual needs of the plaintiff—for example, monthly payments with periodic increases or various "balloon" payments at specified times for anticipated needs, such as college expenses. Structured settlements also have the advantage of preserving large monetary settlements from dissipation by plaintiffs who are unprepared to manage large sums of money.

Because most structured settlement offers involve more than straight-line annuity calculations, it is often difficult to determine the actual present value or cost of specific lump-sum payments, coupled with varying amounts of fixed payments, based on one or more life expectancies. To give an informed opinion on the viability of a proposed structured settlement to a client, a lawyer may need to consult with an economist who can perform computer analyses of the entire proposed settlement, including its tax implications. In addition, software, such as the "Structured Settlement" program in the PC Economist series, can provide useful assistance.

F. "REALISTIC EXPECTATIONS" AND AUTHORITY

1. ARRIVING AT "REALISTIC EXPECTATIONS"

As discussed previously, before entering into negotiations on behalf of a client, a lawyer should discuss with the client on an on-going basis, *inter alia*, the strengths and weaknesses of the case, the parties' interests and concerns, the client's BATNA, the "value" of the case, and the planned negotiation strategy in light of the client's interests.

This entire process should lead to the development of what has been termed as "realistic expectations" *before* negotiations begin. In *Smart Negotiating: How to Make Good Deals in the Real World*, James C. Freund explains that "realistic expectations" are "a blend of aspiration and feasibility." According to Freund, the "aspiration" component is what the client "reasonably hope[s] to achieve from the negotiation [based on] a combination of objective elements of value and where [the client] will feel good about the outcome." The "feasibility" component combines the estimate of what the opposing party wants to achieve with "the relative weight of the various leverage factors present."

Freund points out that this determination of realistic expectations will have to be made based only on estimates, but "an imperfect determination is better than none at all."

2. OBTAINING AUTHORITY FROM THE CLIENT

In addition, before the negotiation begins, the lawyer and client should consider the extent of the lawyer's authority to enter into a binding agreement on behalf of the client. It is widely recommended that lawyers obtain this authority in writing. The need for this written authorization can be explained to clients on the ground that it is necessary to prevent any misunderstandings. Professor Jacker suggests another justification is that it would undermine the other side's confidence in future offers if an erroneous one was made and had to be withdrawn.

When authority is given orally to lawyers, it is good practice to confirm that authority in writing— provided sufficient time exists for that purpose. The confirming letter should request that the client immediately inform the lawyer if there is any misunderstanding. When insufficient time exists for a confirming letter, the instruction given to the lawyer should be reviewed with the client and orally confirmed. Professor Jacker points out that lawyers should be especially cautious about acting on authority provided through a telephone message taken by another person.

One type of authority is *unlimited authority*, which allows the negotiator to enter into any agreement on behalf of the client. Many commentators, however, warn that a lawyer should be especially wary of clients who say, in effect, "Do whatever you think best." As discussed previously, the lawyer needs to work with the client to avoid lawyer dominance of the client-counseling process, including making decisions about negotiations. Another type of authority is *open authority*, which allows the lawyer to negotiate but leaves the final approval necessary to create a binding agreement with the client.

Another type of authority is *limited authority*. Professor Gifford's article, *The Synthesis of Legal Counseling and Negotiation Models: Preserving Client-Centered Advocacy in the Negotiation Context*, points out that one advantage of limited authority is that it encourages clients to retain greater control over their lawyer's conduct during the negotiation. Gifford notes that "[a] series of incrementally increasing grants of authority over the course of the negotiation guarantees that the [lawyer] must consult regularly with the client." In this way, the lawyer will be encouraged to "preface such requests for additional authority with reports on the current status of the negotiations," and as a result the lawyer will "keep the client better informed about the negotiations and more directly involved in them."

It is widely noted that many clients, particularly insurance companies, prefer to set relatively tight limits on authority. This approach has the advantage of possibly enhancing negotiator toughness because the negotiator, in reality, does not have the authority to concede. It allows the negotiator to respond with honesty and conviction. It also avoids the ethical problem of possibly having to lie about the authority that has been granted.

When authority has been granted, the negotiator may become liable for the failure to make an offer. For example, in *Smiley v. Manchester Insurance & Indemnity Co.* (1978), an insurance defense lawyer was negligent as a matter of law and was liable for the amount of the verdict against the insurer in excess of the policy limits for failing to communicate an authorized offer to the plaintiff's lawyer.

G. DRAFTING PROPOSED AGREEMENTS PRIOR TO NEGOTIATIONS

In terms of actually preparing a draft of an agreement to present to the other side, Professor Norbert Jacker in his videotape, *Negotiation Techniques for the Trial Advocate,* suggests the following approach. A lawyer should try to find the first draft of a similar agreement prepared from the client's perspective—for example, from the buyer's perspective if the client is the buyer. Using that draft and favorable items from the final agreement, the negotiator should then prepare a draft. The negotiator could then submit that draft for comments to relevant persons, such as a tax specialist, an antitrust lawyer, or an estate planner.

At this point, Professor Jacker recommends the "creative use of colored pencils," by using a different colored pencil to record the comments of each person on a master copy. In this way, the lawyer will be able to keep track of who suggested the changes. Word processing programs can perform the same functions by means of "track changes," "redline," or "comments" tools.

After the changes have been made, the revised copy could be circulated for further review. Professor Jacker suggests that the drafts not be numbered consecutively (Draft No. 1, Draft No. 2, and so on). Instead, a date could be used so that a person receiving the equivalent of Draft No. 3 does not wonder why they have not received earlier drafts.

After the draft has been finalized, the lawyer then can send the draft to the client for review. In a corporate setting, several persons may be involved, such as officers, technical and marketing personnel, accountants, and others. The same colored pencil technique or word processing methods can be used to keep track of their respective comments and changes. The draft can then be submitted for the first time to the other side. Professor Jacker recommends that a cover letter should indicate that the draft is also being reviewed by the lawyer's own client and that there may be changes.

On the other hand, if a draft from the other side is received, Professor Jacker suggests that the draft be circulated in the same manner for review and comment. To maintain control of the drafting process if there are extensive changes, Professor Jacker recommends that the draft be retyped on the lawyer's word processor and then resubmitted to the other side. An appropriate cover letter could indicate that because of the changes, it was easier to have the entire document retyped.

H. NEGOTIATION NOTES AND NOTEBOOKS

Several commentators suggest that it is critically important to keep detailed notes, memos, and records of each conversation or meeting. For example, in his book, *Friendly Persuasion: My Life as a Negotiator*, Bob Woolf gives a good illustration of the value of keeping careful notes, especially when the negotiations are conducted over the telephone. Woolf was representing a meteorologist and was conducting a contract negotiation with a television station manager. In the first conversation, the station manager twice emphatically indicated that the station would never go above a salary of $120,000.

Two days later, the station manager insisted that "under no circumstances will I go beyond $120,000. That's it." Woolf again called back at the end of the week. The station manager again snapped: "Why are you still calling me? I told you, my best offer is $120,000. That's it." Woolf waited two more weeks. This time, the station manager said, "You're wasting your breath. I told you, *$140,000* is as far as I'm going to go." Apparently, the station manager "had been wading through an usually hectic month and had failed to write down the figure." As Woolf concludes, "my notes were better than his."

Others recommend a more comprehensive approach to organize the preparation for a negotiation and to record its progression. For example, in the essential legal skills book, *Negotiation*, Diana Tribe recommends creating a "negotiation notebook"—a binder with divisions and subdivisions for each of the following items:

Section A. Overview (including list of issues in dispute which are to be negotiated, a clear statement as to the client's preferred outcomes, and time chart);

Section B. Facts and Figures (including documents, reports, receipts, factual deficiencies that need to be explored or remedied, notes on meeting dates, telephone conversations, and applicable legal rules or authorities, etc.);

Section C. Advance Planning and Detailed Preparation (including general matters concerning the characteristics and preferences of the other negotiator, prioritized agenda items, planned style and strategy, authority, an analysis of strengths and weakness, potential rebuttals, possible creative solutions, details of objective criteria, planned concessions, etc.); and

Section D. Negotiation Meeting Notes (notes recording the progress of the negotiation, tentative agreements, etc.).

CHAPTER 4

OPENING THE NEGOTIATION, BARGAINING, INFORMATION EXCHANGE, TACTICS, AND PERSUASION

The general relationship between a negotiator's approach in terms of strategy and style affects bargaining, the information exchange, tactics, and ultimately the results. Professor Menkel-Meadow graphically summarizes this relationship as follows:

Orientation → Mind set → Behavior →Results.

This chapter blends together a variety of considerations and patterns that reflect these basic choices. It also deals with certain underlying problems, such as surveillance and publicity, truth in legal negotiations, and legal limits on intimidation.

A. ENVIRONMENTAL CONSIDERATIONS AND PRELIMINARY MATTERS

Legal negotiation is influenced by a variety of important considerations, including the actual means or method of negotiating—for example, face-to-face negotiation versus over the telephone; the location of the negotiation; its physical setting; timing; the parties involved; and the agenda. Many of these items will be established prior to or at the beginning of a negotiating session.

1. LOCATION

The location of a negotiation—and other procedural details as well—are often the subject of preliminary negotiations between the parties. The site of the negotiations is often a matter of considerable contention in international negotiations. The classic example is the Communists' insistence on holding the Korean War peace conference in the "demilitarized" zone on the 38th parallel rather than on a neutral noncombatant ship at sea as proposed by the United Nations negotiators. Only after the peace conference had commenced did the United Nations negotiators realize the conference site was actually in a combat zone under Communist control.

In a more typical legal context, the choice is ordinarily between negotiating at one's own office (or that of the lawyer's client), the other negotiator's office (or that of the opposing party), or some neutral location, such as the judge's chambers or other neutral office space. In considering the location of a legal negotiation, there are widely recognized advantages and disadvantages to negotiating at one's own office or the other negotiator's office.

a. Being the Host

Hosting the negotiation is said to be preferable for several reasons. First, the location of the negotiations may reflect the physical arrangements and psychological climate at that site. Generally speaking, the host of negotiations has a legitimate right to assume responsibility for arranging the physical setting—often to the host's "competitive" advantage. In sports, this aspect is referred to as the "home field advantage." In contrast, when the negotiation occurs at a neutral site, the physical arrangements are normally decided upon by mutual consent of the negotiators.

Second, the guest-host relationship may subtly influence the negotiators to take on dominant-subordinate roles in which the host is more assertive and the guest more deferential than would occur at a neutral site. Magnanimously making the visiting negotiator comfortable—offering coffee or arranging for food, for example—has the advantage of subtly highlighting the host negotiator's power.

Third, controlling the physical setting has the advantage of creating a pleasant setting which improves the other negotiator's mood. Studies suggest that a good mood on the part of the negotiator may enhance concession making.

Fourth, if agreement is reached at a site that the negotiator controls, it allows the negotiator the option of dictating a memorandum of agreement or preparing other documents immediately for signature.

Fifth, the negotiator often saves traveling time and expense and imposes them on the other side. The fatigue and stress resulting from travel may also be a factor that works to one's advantage. Another practical consequence is that the host negotiator may immediately memorialize the information obtained in the negotiation—perhaps in greater detail than otherwise would be possible if time was spent traveling before completing this task.

b. Being the Guest

On the other hand, not hosting the negotiation is said to have several advantages. First, negotiating elsewhere may provide the opportunity to avoid turning over information that would otherwise be readily accessible if the negotiation took place at the negotiator's office. Likewise, it creates the opportunity for the negotiator to "forget" to bring information or other items.

Second, negotiating elsewhere makes it easier to break off negotiations by finding an excuse to leave. For example, if the negotiation turns to a topic that a visiting negotiator does not want to discuss, it is easier to tell the other lawyer that you must leave than it is for the host negotiator to tell the visiting negotiator to leave. In this way, the visiting negotiator gains greater control over the timing.

Third, negotiating elsewhere creates the opportunity to take advantage of problems that occur at the host negotiator's office. For example, the guest negotiator can be magnanimous when interruptions occur. The guest negotiator also gains psychologically when the host is unable to provide a requested item. For example, if the host negotiator offers coffee or a soft drink and, in response, the guest negotiator asks for mineral water or hot tea, the host negotiator must suffer the embarrassment of being unable to make the guest negotiator comfortable.

2. THE PHYSICAL SETTING

Two principal aspects of the physical setting are (a) seating arrangements and (b) climatic conditions and availability of other amenities. The physical setting for the negotiation may have an important effect on the atmosphere of the negotiation and the relationship of the negotiators.

A classic example of the psychological importance of seating and the physical setting is related by Michael Meltsner and Philip Schrag in their book, *Public Interest Advocacy: Materials for Clinical Legal Education.* In Charlie Chaplin's film, *The Great Dictator*, Adolph Hitler has invited Benito Mussolini to Germany to decide whether Italy or Germany will invade a neutral country. Hitler's aides arrange for Mussolini to enter Hitler's long office from the end opposite the desk. Mussolini will thus have to walk a long way to reach Hitler and will naturally feel small in Hitler's enormous office. Hitler's aides also have provided a specially constructed chair for Mussolini. The extremely low chair will force Mussolini to look up at Hitler. Mussolini, however, enters by the back door. He calmly sits on Hitler's desk and looks down at Hitler. They then continue the negotiation in a barber shop—where the dictators compete with each other during the negotiations by continually raising their respective barber chairs to achieve additional height.

a. Seating

The seating arrangements are probably the most important aspect of the physical setting of the negotiation. Ordinarily, a neutral kind of seating arrangement is one in which every negotiator has roughly the same kind of seat, view, and access to other members of their respective negotiating teams (A-B-C vs. D-E-F).

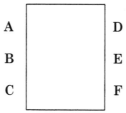

If an opposing negotiator makes or attempts to make variations from a neutral arrangement, it is likely an attempt to gain a competitive advantage. Furthermore, although disputes over physical arrangements (seating arrangements, name plates, or the use of flags) may seem trivial and independent of the substantive issues involved, they may be important expressions of less tangible sources of contention, such as the relative power and status of the negotiating parties. This aspect of setting the procedural ground rules often arises in international disputes. A classic example is the prolonged negotiation over the arrangement of the tables and chairs at the Paris Vietnam peace talks.

Seating arrangements may have subtle effects on the relationship of the negotiators. Face-to-face seating is widely regarded as more conducive to confrontational behavior. It may also be the preferred arrangement when a negotiator seeks to obtain information from the other negotiator but does not want to establish a friendly relationship.

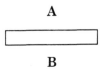

On the other hand, side-by-side seating is generally viewed as more conducive to cooperative relationships and information sharing.

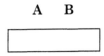

Similarly, seating at right angles at square or rectangular tables generally facilitates a more cooperative relationship than face-to-face seating.

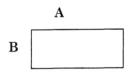

Seating arrangements may also be used to control the formality of the negotiating session and the amount of tension or relaxation aroused in the participants. For example, when the physical arrangements inappropriately impose or require physical or visual contact, then tension, defensiveness, and conflict intensity are likely to increase. On the other hand, round-shaped tables are widely thought to increase informality and feelings of closeness compared to square or rectangular tables. Furthermore, seating arrangements may affect a person's apparent authority—the person at the head of the table has a natural psychological advantage in terms of control.

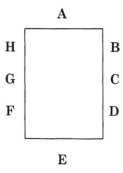

In psychological terms, the power status flows clockwise around the table: A, in the twelve o'clock or chief position is the "head" of the table; H is the weakest position; E is the seat likely to be chosen for direct opposition to A.

Seating arrangements may help establish what is traditionally termed a "good guy-bad guy" relationship. The "good guy-bad guy" approach involves making one of the negotiators on one side of the negotiation appear to be the "bad guy" (A) by acting hostile and unreasonable—refusing to accept the other side's requests. Another person on the same side plays the role of a "good guy" (C)—who is reasonable and willing to give the other side what they want. When this tactic is used, the good guy can try to sit with the opposing party. This physical arrangement helps associate the good guy (C) with the opposing party (B).

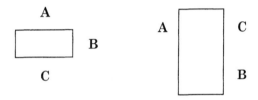

Cultural differences provide variations in the size and importance of personal space. In planning the physical setting for the negotiation, it should be remembered that people can be inadvertently annoyed by sitting or standing too close or too far from other participants in the negotiation.

b. *Climatic Conditions and Other Amenities*

Other aspects of the physical setting are important. Items that hinder effective communication—and thus should be avoided—include interruptions, unpleasant climatic conditions (*e.g.*, like excessive heat), lack of amenities, and noise. Provision should be made for reasonable breaks, refreshments, food, and other amenities. People who are physically uncomfortable are less likely to be agreeable.

3. TIME CONSIDERATIONS

Time considerations are sometimes addressed in preliminary negotiations. These time considerations include (1) the time at which the negotiators will meet; (2) the length of the negotiating session(s); and (3) the deadline for reaching an agreement, if any. As a general matter, if no discernible progress is made within the first few hours of a negotiating session, it is widely thought to be best to recess or schedule a future session because experience shows that significant progress is unlikely. An exception might be when the parties are approaching a significant deadline.

Negotiators have different energy cycles or biological rhythms—times when they are apt to perform the best, such as the morning. Negotiators should be aware of their own personal cycles and should attempt to schedule negotiations during times in which they perform at their best. When a negotiator travels, time differences (and accompanying jet lag) should likewise be taken into account.

In a litigation context, Professor Williams suggests that the litigation process can be used to increase perceived time pressures once litigation has been commenced. By conducting the litigation efficiently and keeping the litigation constantly on the mind of opposing counsel, pressure on the other side can be created to prepare and encourage early determination of the dispute. As a collateral benefit, such negotiators enhance their reputation in terms of toughness and credibility—both in the eyes of the opponents and their own clients.

During Stage One (Orientation and Positioning), discussed in Chapter 2(F), above, Professor Williams suggests that a lawyer should stay active and working on the case. The lawyer should avoid using boilerplate interrogatories, needless motions, and other dilatory tactics. The lawyer should insist with the judge on early scheduling of all conferences and the trial date. Similarly, Professor Williams recommends that the lawyer put the judge and the other lawyer on notice that the lawyer intends to be prepared and expects the other lawyer to be prepared also. The lawyer should routinely and consistently find reasons and methods for keeping in active communication with the other side. Furthermore, the lawyer should set a good example by always being prompt in returning phone calls, being prompt in keeping appointments, and being fastidious in correspondence.

Professor Williams also suggests that Stage One is the time to establish a nonthreatening atmosphere that invites cooperation by making "free concessions." One way to appear to be cooperative during the initial stages is to promise to cooperate to work out the best possible solution. The lawyer can also promise to be willing to negotiate and to make real concessions when the time is right. The lawyer can give empathy. Professor Williams points out that it costs the lawyer nothing to show reasonable sympathy for and understanding of the opposing party's needs and problems. It creates good will and a cooperative atmosphere.

However, if the lawyer's approach is an adversarial one, the lawyer should make no substantive concessions during Stage One.

4. THE PARTIES INVOLVED, SURVEILLANCE, AND PUBLICITY

When there is a multi-party dispute in which several persons or groups have a stake in the outcome of the negotiation, some preliminary agreement will need to be reached on (1) who will be present during the negotiation, including neutral persons, experts, and other third parties; and (2) who will be conducting the negotiation. Represented individuals or groups will need to determine the extent of their involvement in the decision-making process. In some instances, affected parties will have to be given notice and an opportunity to participate or be represented.

In their book, *Public Interest Advocacy: Materials for Clinical Legal Education,* Michael Meltsner and Philip Schrag suggest that a negotiator should attempt to determine or estimate the number of persons the other side will be bringing to the negotiating session. They maintain that the negotiator should try to have an equal number or possibly one more person present. They reason that a side with fewer representatives will tire more easily and will be less able to control the flow of the discussion. Furthermore, they suggest that there is a tendency to reach a compromise that is evenly balanced among the views of all the participants—thus, the active presence of additional negotiators materially affects the outcome.

Other commentators discourage "ganging up" on the other side. Indeed, Meltsner and Schrag state that the presence of additional representatives should be justified on some ground, such as the need to have present technical expertise necessary to complete the negotiation. Otherwise, as Meltsner and Schrag recognize, the opposing side may feel "cornered."

Legal negotiation inherently involves "surveillance" by various "audiences"—persons or groups who directly observe a legal negotiation or who will learn of a negotiator's conduct and performance. That audience often can reward or punish the negotiator based on the performance and outcome.

In a legal negotiation, several types of audiences are possible. First, the audience may be directly affected by the outcome, such as a defendant in plea bargaining or the employees in a labor-management negotiation. Second, the audience may have an indirect interest in achieving a settlement, but not in the particular outcome. For example, the judge before whom the lawsuit is pending has an interest in getting the case off the docket, but not necessarily an interest in what the specific terms are. Third, the audience may not have any vested interest in the outcome or in achieving a settlement—most often the press or other media.

Negotiation research shows that the presence—physically or psychologically—of audiences can have an important effect on negotiation behavior. First, when an audience is present, negotiators are motivated to seek positive (and avoid negative) evaluations from that audience, particularly if the audience is an important client constituency. Negotiators want to please their clients. At the same time, the presence of the audience heightens the negotiator's concern about image loss.

Second, the presence of an audience generates pressure toward stronger loyalty, commitment, and advocacy of the audience's preferred positions that may interfere with reaching a settlement. One possible way around this problem is to hold informal discussions outside the formal negotiation channels so that the rhetoric can be avoided. The formal positions are left intact while the negotiators are given a freer opportunity to discuss options and possible solutions.

Third, the presence of a judge or a mediator may increase pressure toward agreement. The judge or mediator may also reduce irrationality, facilitate communication, and limit unethical behavior.

Because of the significant effects of surveillance of negotiations, some "ground rules" are often established concerning publicity. Thus, a preliminary decision will have to be made (1) whether the negotiations will be public or private; (2) how and when information will be released to the public or interested groups; and (3) who will make those releases. In some instances, of course, the negotiations may have to be held in public because of sunshine legislation.

5. NEGOTIATING FORMAT

Another matter that will need to be established by preliminary negotiations is the actual means or method of formally negotiating the dispute—for example, exchange of letters, face-to-face negotiation, or discussion over the telephone. Determining the method of formally negotiating can involve varying negotiation methods itself.

Communication, of course, can occur on both a verbal and nonverbal level. Indeed, actions (and reactions) often speak louder than words; thus, important information can be learned by observing head nods, facial expressions, and gestures. The opportunity to observe these nonverbal forms of communication, however, is lost when negotiation is conducted on the telephone. Furthermore, when a lawyer is negotiating on the telephone, it is sometimes difficult to tell whether the other party's attention is being directed elsewhere. For example, the other party's attention may become immediately focused on the presence of a supervising partner just when the other party is communicating an important point.

In general, lawyers should negotiate important matters in person, not over the telephone. Telephone negotiations make it easy to say "no." Hanging up ends communication. Telephone negotiations also tend to be much shorter than person-to-person negotiations. It is widely believed that negotiators with relatively weak positions should especially avoid telephone negotiations. Telephone negotiations generally are regarded as more competitive than a face-to-face meeting and the stronger position tends to prevail among negotiators using a competitive style.

It is generally thought also that the initiator of the call has the advantage. The caller can prepare. The recipient of an unexpected call thus might be caught off guard and not fully prepared. If a lawyer is the recipient of an unexpected call, the lawyer may want to find an excuse to return the call. Using silence, particularly if it is an international long-distance call, may induce the other party to fill the gap by talking; a lawyer is likely to obtain useful information from the caller.

In preparing for a telephone negotiation, it is often suggested that a lawyer should make a checklist of items or points to be covered. At the same time, the lawyer should have needed facts and figures readily available. If figures are involved, a lawyer should have a calculator close at hand. It is also widely recommended that the lawyer prepare a memorandum dealing with the agreements reached in an important telephone conversation.

6. NEGOTIATING AGENDA

"Ground rules" also frequently cover the items to be negotiated. Depending on the circumstances, some items may be designated as nonnegotiable and not to be discussed. Another ground rule may cover how and when new matters may be raised for negotiation. The relationship of the items being negotiated may also be established. It is often said that "stacking the agenda" is a way of gaining tactical advantage. Professor Jacker suggests that one way to gain such an advantage is to present a printed or typed agenda, particularly when the issues are complex. Like other preliminary matters, agenda items may consume considerable time in international negotiations.

7. SINGLE NEGOTIATING TEXT

Another possible "ground rule" is for the parties to decide to use what Fisher and Ury call a "single negotiating text," particularly in a transactional setting. This approach involves the use of a third-party mediator who listens to each party's needs, concerns, and interests. The mediator then draws up a list of those needs, concerns, and interests for review and additional suggestions. Based on this input, the mediator then drafts a proposal—the single negotiating text—for review by both sides. Based on further input from the parties, this process continues until the parties either accept or reject the proposed agreement.

Fisher and Ury suggest that several advantages flow from this arrangement. The focus of the negotiation is on the parties' interests rather than their positions. The process also assists the parties in setting priorities and reduces the number of decisions that the parties have to make in order to reach an agreement. Furthermore, the mediator may help generate innovative solutions to bridge the gaps that may be revealed. On the other hand, this approach can be time consuming and is dependent on the skills of the mediator. Furthermore, the risk exists that one party may decide to deal elsewhere and terminate the process before agreement is reached.

B. OPENING THE NEGOTIATION AND MAKING OPENING OFFERS

As noted previously, a common characteristic of effective legal negotiators is being prepared. Unpreparedness weakens your negotiating position and lessens your opponent's respect for you as a negotiator and litigator. Preparation includes researching the facts and the law, formulating arguments and counterarguments, knowing the tax consequences involved, assessing case value accurately, and considering integrative, problem-solving solutions. Preparation also includes planning a negotiating strategy and style.

As discussed in Chapter 2, negotiating style can be seen as a continuum —with the pure cooperative style and tactics at one extreme and the pure competitive style and tactics at the other. Common experience suggests that every person can shift from one style and set of tactics to another under sufficient encouragement or provocation—in other words, everyone can move on this continuum one direction or another. Effective trial lawyers engage in some degree of acting at trial and so do law professors in the classroom. Some degree of acting and planned strategy may likewise be called for in legal negotiation in the course of the argumentation phase, concession making, and search for alternative solutions that takes place in Stage Two of the negotiation process. Cooperatives are particularly prone to believe that it is dishonest to calculate which role to play and that the honest person must respond "naturally" to a situation rather than plan in advance how to gain an advantage.

When the parties are at the bargaining table and the ground rules have been established, one of the parties will "open" the negotiation. Several commentators suggest that the opening remarks should be carefully chosen because they can strongly influence the other party's perception and create a positive or negative atmosphere. As discussed in the preceding chapter, the opening part of a negotiation provides the opportunity to establish positions or to convey information about the goals, concerns, and needs of the parties. The approach taken will be influenced by the negotiator's basic strategy.

If an adversarial strategy is adopted, an important part of convincing the opponent that a negotiator has a strong case (and that substantial concessions must be made to resolve it) is attempting to influence the opponent's view of the value of the case. If the negotiator represents the plaintiff, a negotiator using an adversarial strategy should begin with a relatively high level of demands. Conversely, if such a negotiator represents the defendant, the negotiator should establish a relatively tough position favorable to the defendant.

In an adversarial context, this approach is essentially a maximalist one. Studies indicate that bargainers who were unsure of the value of the case tend to use the opponent's opening bid to set their own goals in the case. A maximal opening offer enhances settlement value because it raises (or lowers) the psychological mid-point between the opening positions. It also protects the negotiator against the danger of committing to an overly modest evaluation of the case and it hides the negotiator's real or minimum expectations and at the same time creates negotiating "currency."

Professor Williams warns that negotiators should avoid the temptation of trying to short-circuit the negotiation ritual. For example, some insurance defense lawyers (having long represented insurers) develop a certain disdain for plaintiff's lawyers. Rather than going through the ritual of the stages of negotiation, certain insurance defense lawyers will use their specialized expertise and experience to place a fair value on the case. At some point during the early development, they will inform the plaintiff's lawyer of that value. Thereafter, they will refuse to negotiate, to be convinced, or to give the plaintiff's lawyer the satisfaction of wringing concessions from them. This approach, in effect, is take-it-or-leave-it —meaning, take the first offer or go to trial. Because the plaintiff's lawyer is unable to deliver a better offer to the client—despite further discovery, time, and expense—the defendant's take-it-or-leave-it approach forces the plaintiff's lawyer (for face saving and other reasons) to recommend trial to the plaintiff, even though the original settlement offer was a "fair" one.

The defense lawyer in an adversarial negotiation would be better served by starting low and then making concessions. The effect will be to induce the plaintiff to expect less because the defense lawyer would not have created high expectations with a "fair" first offer. This approach will also make the plaintiff feel that the lawyer's efforts are paying dividends. Not only will more cases settle, but they will settle at a better result for the defense lawyer. It will also result in more satisfied plaintiffs and plaintiffs' lawyers. Perhaps a take-it-or-leave-it approach might be justified against an extremely weak opponent if it is accompanied by a full explanation. Even then, however, the opponent may react negatively.

As discussed in the preceding chapters, a negotiator using a problem-solving approach would draw upon planning that has taken place prior to entering the negotiation. That planning should have included an assessment of the parties' underlying economic, legal, social, psychological, and ethical concerns and needs, both in the short run and the long run. That planning should have also included a careful investigation of possible solutions and resources. The negotiator will try to establish the legitimacy of the client's interests and focus the discussion on the needs and concerns of the parties.

Fisher and Ury recommend active listening and acknowledgment of the opposing party's concerns. Opening positions are typically probed with "why" questions. Menkel-Meadow suggests that a negotiator using a problem-solving approach can still try to solve problems even when the opposing side emphasizes an adversarial strategy or competitive tactics. Problem solving will be "closed" when the other parties' needs are blocked and information is not shared. Nonetheless, a problem-solving negotiator can still strive for solutions to meet the parties' apparent but perhaps incomplete and possibly inaccurate needs.

The opening offer pattern of a negotiator using a problem-solving strategy is likely to contrast with the opening offer pattern of a negotiator using an adversarial strategy. Bastress and Harbaugh point out that the pertinent question for problem-solving negotiators is not "how much" the opening offer should be, but "how many" opening offers or possible solutions should be simultaneously made. Indeed, the problem-solving negotiator will treat making multiple offers as an important aspect of overall strategy to influence an opponent using an adversarial strategy to adopt a joint problem-solving approach. Multiple offers or solutions force the other negotiator to respond to the offers in ways that are likely to clarify the opponent's needs. Multiple offers or solutions help expose feigned needs. Avoiding the use of a single offer also helps avoid the linear argumentation and concession pattern characteristic of adversarial negotiations. A key aspect of making multiple offers or proposals is assessing the response in terms of exposing or meeting a real need of the other party.

According to Bastress and Harbaugh, negotiators using a problem-solving strategy are less likely to be concerned about who makes the opening offer. When a competitive or cooperative problem solver negotiates with a person following an adversarial strategy, it is suggested that the problem solver is more likely to make the first offers. When a cooperative problem solver negotiates with a competitive problem solver, Bastress and Harbaugh indicate that the cooperative problem solver is likely to initiate the offer process in an open and broad fashion—with the competitive problem solver holding back and preferring to react. To be effective, they suggest that the cooperative problem solver must demand that the competitive problem solver analyze all resolutions suggested, not just those advantageous to the competitive problem solver's side.

C. PRESENTING A FAVORABLE CONCEPTUALIZATION OF THE CASE, MAKING ARGUMENTS, AND SEARCHING FOR SOLUTIONS

As discussed in Chapter 2(F), during Stage Two ("Argumentation, Compromise, and Search for Alternative Solutions") of the stages in an adversarial negotiation, the negotiators attempt to move each other away from their respective opening positions and toward a more reasonable or favorable position. During this and the next stage ("Emergence and Crisis"), communication of arguments, characterization of the facts, and bargaining effectiveness will determine how far each side will be willing to move to reach agreement.

1. CONCEPTUALIZING THE FACTS

One of the most valuable characteristics of effective trial and appellate lawyers is the ability to conceptualize the facts in favorable ways. That ability is no less important to a legal negotiator. It is widely recognized among effective advocates that "cases are what you make of them" and that cases themselves do not have one inherent, intrinsic value, but instead a range of values.

In an adversarial context, one way of supporting a higher (or lower) case value is by characterizing the facts in their strategically most favorable light—portraying a favorable jury and how the case might be presented to them. In conceptualizing the case, the negotiator thus needs to paint a picture with enough credibility to raise the fear in the opponent that what is projected—although perhaps only remotely possible—*might just happen.*

As discussed in Chapter 2, the basic dynamic of the cooperative style is to move psychologically toward the opposing party. Cooperatives communicate a sense of shared interests, values, and attitudes. They seek common ground and promote a trusting atmosphere. They use rational, logical persuasion as a means of seeking cooperation. Professor Williams found that competitive negotiators interpret this cooperation as a sign of weakness. From the viewpoint of a competitive negotiator, people who are strong and people with strong cases do not make concessions or admit to weaknesses. When an opponent acts cooperatively with them, competitive negotiators actually *increase* their level of demands and their expectations about what they will be able to obtain in the case. Failure to make a vigorous defense of a negotiating position or showing undue concern about the cost of reaching no agreement can cause an image loss and increased demands by competitive negotiators.

Thus, in an adversarial context, every time a negotiator's conceptualization of the case or the legal negotiator's position is called into question, the negotiator must convincingly defend it. The negotiator must come up with counterarguments or retorts. The negotiator has to find ways to deal with weaknesses. Negotiators with cooperative tendencies often expect that, if they say something once, their opponents should believe them. Once, however, is not enough to establish and defend a position convincingly and vigorously. Professor Williams suggests that a negotiator must respond as many times with convincing sincerity as the negotiator's position is called into question. Otherwise, if the negotiator passively absorbs attacks on the negotiator's position (or the negotiator personally), *the negotiator will actually encourage escalating demands and aggressive tactics*—while upgrading the opponent's expectations. A tough defense will help demonstrate the strength of the case, convince the opponent that the negotiator is a formidable opponent with no identifiable weaknesses, and present a case with every likelihood of winning on the merits.

On the other hand, if a negotiator fails to establish and maintain a position in this way in an adversarial negotiation and then compromises, the negotiator will be dealing from a position of weakness, not strength, when real compromises are made. Professor Williams also recommends avoiding the trap of withholding the "best" facts to surprise the other side at trial. Remember that for any group of ten cases, nine of them are likely to be settled without a trial. By reserving the best facts for trial, the negotiator is in the awkward position of arguing for a value on the case that is not fully supported.

The process of developing a favorable conceptualization of the case and defending a position vigorously has another important benefit in an adversarial negotiation. It helps create and reinforce the negotiator's own expectations for favorable outcome—high or low, depending on whom the negotiator represents. Developing and internalizing those high expectations goes hand-in-hand with a convincing and sincere presentation in an adversarial negotiation.

Effectiveness in legal negotiation requires presenting the issues in a strategically favorable light and selectively controlling the flow of information. Facts are not purely neutral. They are subject to legitimate characterization in much the same way as they would be presented to a jury. Thus, prior to negotiating, it is critically important for a negotiator using an adversarial strategy to consider how to conceptualize and interpret the facts in ways to enhance a negotiator's position.

Furthermore, this conceptualization must be communicated and "driven home" to the other side during the negotiation. In other words, a negotiator should not "simply let the facts fend for themselves." Indeed, it is a mark of an effective negotiator who "paints the picture" with sincerity, conviction, and forthrightness as many times as that picture is called into question. On the other hand, it is often suggested that a negotiator should avoid repeating unchallenged statements more than twice.

2. ADJUSTING THE ORDER OF PRESENTING ARGUMENTS

With cooperative opponents in an adversarial negotiation, a legal negotiator can appear to be more cooperative by starting with areas that minimize the differences between the clients and by seeking to establish common ground and cooperative exchanges. With competitive opponents, however, Professor Williams suggests that it is probably best to emphasize differences and to present the strongest and most convincing arguments first. Professor Williams also found that effective competitive negotiators create false issues (ones that have no real importance to that side but are made to seem important for purposes of later trading them for concessions).

3. MAKING ARGUMENTS AND GAME PLAYING

Two aspects about making arguments and counterarguments should be carefully considered: (1) supporting positions with "evidence" rather than rhetoric and (2) avoiding or breaking through "game playing."

a. Supporting Positions with "Evidence"

Many commentators suggest that the best approach to making arguments in a legal negotiation is to present "evidence" in support of a position or view. By presenting evidence and reasons, a legal negotiator's position takes on increased credibility. For example, in an adversarial negotiation, a negotiator may present evidence of the value of the case, the lack of time pressure, or the inability to make further concessions. In presenting this evidence in support of a position, the negotiator should avoid negative elements, such as flat assertions and contradictory emotions. They convey the impression that the issue is closed to examination and reduce the other negotiator's receptivity.

Commentators have also observed that argument spacing is important. A negotiator should provide enough space between presenting ideas and arguments to allow the other negotiator to absorb them fully. More time is needed for complex proposals, ideas, or arguments. Simple examples are a good way to reinforce the arguments presented. As discussed below, visual aids can substantially enhance the presentation of arguments. Likewise, organized materials, such as settlement brochures, have the advantage of a cumulative impact.

b. *Communication Game Playing*

To make up for preparation and evidence supporting a position and to gain advantage through one-upmanship, there is a tendency in negotiation to engage in what various commentators call "communication game playing." In transactional analysis terms, game playing often involves "parent-child" communication rather than "adult-to-adult" communication. The reason for avoiding game playing is that it jeopardizes the negotiation process by promoting distrust. It also destroys rapport and inhibits the cooperation necessary to attain objectives.

Generally speaking, game playing can be recognized when a person feels discounted or believes that the negotiation is not getting anywhere. The basic cues are the various forms of "should," "ought," "do," "don't," and "be like me" associated with the parent role in transactional analysis. Many forms of intimidation also involve this type of communication.

Researchers and commentators have identified a large number of different kinds of games, many of which are directly relevant to legal negotiation. For example, one kind of game involves *expertise*. In this game, the negotiator tries in various ways to establish a position of credibility and dominance over the other negotiator on the ground that the negotiator knows more than the other. In other words, the negotiator has "superior" knowledge and understanding of the law or facts. This expertise (which, in fact, may be completely lacking) is often the justification for a take-it-or-leave-it position.

Another kind of game involves facts and figures—the so-called *snow job* game. In this game, the negotiator tries to overwhelm the other negotiator with an abundance of conclusionary facts and figures. When the negotiator is asked to explain or provide detailed support, the negotiator refuses on the ground that it is unnecessary and the facts speak for themselves (perhaps implying that the other negotiator is dumb for not understanding).

Still another kind of game is the so-called "*wooden leg*" game. In this game, a negotiator argues that a limitation excuses the rejection of a reasonable proposal or position or otherwise makes the negotiator not responsible for the situation (*"What would you expect from a person with a wooden leg?"*). Applying this kind of game to labor-management negotiations, for example, a union will sometimes use a purported lack of financial resources and staff to prepare for negotiations (its "wooden leg") as a basis for not being able to directly counteract a well-documented and well-prepared management presentation.

Closely related to the "wooden leg" game is the *impossible client* game, in which a lawyer claims to understand the other side's position and would like to meet its apparently reasonable demands—except that the impossible client will not let the negotiator do it. In a labor-management context, the negotiator would blame the "unruly mob back at the union hall" or the top management for the inability to accept the proposal at this time.

A "*yes, but*" game occurs when one side appears to be seeking solutions from the other side, but finds a way to deride every solution offered. The true purpose in such a situation is to give "negative strokes" by discounting all the solutions given.

Outrageous behavior is designed to make the other party feel uncomfortable. The purpose of this game or tactic is to induce the uncomfortable party to make a concession in order to stop the outrageous behavior.

A *boredom* game is often played when the opposing side is making its most salient and forceful points or is reiterating points. The negotiator, primarily through body language, sends the message that those points are not impressing the negotiator at all.

"*Funny money*" is sometimes used to make a major decision seem like a small one. This type of game relates small increments of money to small increments of time (*e.g.*, only $1.00 a day over the useful life of the product).

The "*red herring*" is another game or tactic. This game is played when a party throws attention onto a minor issue (the "red herring") and is tough on that issue, then gives in, to get a concession on a major issue.

Still another game is the "*so-what?*" game—a favorite in labor-management negotiations. In this game, immediately after a concession has been won, the side winning will take the position that the item conceded really was not important in the first place—regardless of the priority placed on it prior to the concession.

To break out of such games, several approaches are possible. First, preparation is a key means of avoiding being placed in a child or victim role. Preparation also gives a negotiator the means to direct the discussion to the facts or possible solutions. Second, games require at least two persons to play them and require cooperation to complete them (the delivery of the "negative stroke" or the "put-down"). A negotiator can refuse to cooperate. Third, game playing invites reciprocal game playing. To break out of the game, a negotiator can avoid the temptation to impress or depress the other party. Fourth, a good response is often simply to ignore the behavior and focus on the issues.

4. VISUAL AIDS

Visual aids are an important part of presenting a case effectively to a judge or jury at trial. The same can be true in a legal negotiation. Visual aids include photographs, such as the scene of the accident or injury; copies of official documents, such as police reports; anatomical charts; positive prints of x-rays; models; medical records and reports; letters from doctors to counsel about the injury; letters from employers about work habits and loss of wages; graphs, maps, diagrams, slides and flip charts; computer animations; and other exhibits.

The tactful and proper use of visual aids helps persuade, influence, and increase understanding of opposing parties and their counsel in a way verbal descriptions often fail to do. Even if they are personally unpersuaded, however, the use of visual aids may help them envision how the judge or jury might react to the case. Visual aids also lend credence to the case, help make the negotiator appear prepared, and provide an aura of reasonableness to the demands in an adversarial negotiation.

5. SETTLEMENT BROCHURES

Settlement brochures present a complete history of a case in a factual and readable manner. These brochures typically incorporate visual aids along with a systematic textual presentation of all aspects of the litigation. Many commentators suggest that such a settlement brochure should read like a magazine or a documentary—much like a good motion picture tells a story. Settlement brochures are typically used in personal injury cases, but their use should not be limited to that type of litigation. The process of preparing the brochure may often bolster the negotiator's confidence and preparedness. It also helps create an "aura of legitimacy."

Although the specific content of a settlement brochure varies depending on the aspects of the case and the nature of the claims, the following items are typically suggested for inclusion in a personal injury settlement brochure:

1. Statement of facts, including the client's personal history, injury, treatment, and rehabilitation;

2. Pleadings;

3. Plaintiff's statement;

4. Plaintiff's history;

5. Defendant's history;

6. Summary of the depositions;

7. Demonstrative evidence relating to liability;

8. Summary of trial brief;

9. Summary of medical brief;

10. Exhibits, including documents, photographs, medical reports, instruments, charts, scientific aids, and other similar exhibits;

11. Proposed jury instructions;

12. Local and national jury verdicts relevant to the type of case and injury;

13. Enumerated summary of damages (supported by medical and hospital bills and other enumerated items of past and future expense);

14. Hospital and medical records;

15. Photographs of injuries, including specific injuries, scars, casts, positives of x-rays, and other medical items;

16. Photographs of the plaintiff before injury, including ones showing the client engaged in sporting and social activities;

17. Statements of witnesses;

18. Police reports;

19. Copies of client's tax returns (when relevant);

20. Statements from the client's employer, attending or consulting physicians, and fellow employees; and

21. A brief setting out liability based on points and authorities and your arguments.

The items included in the settlement brochure should be indexed or covered in a table of contents. If an adversarial strategy is being used, it is generally suggested that specific values be set on each portion of the injury rather than setting a general value for the whole case.

In terms of timing, the brochure is often presented after all of the facts are most likely available and the injury has stabilized. A cover letter or introduction is typically used to place conditions on the use of the brochure, to provide for its return, and to limit the evidentiary use of its contents. A settlement brochure can also be coupled with a demand letter for the policy limits.

6. USING THE CLIENT

Despite their general effectiveness, visual aids and settlement brochures may fail to demonstrate fully the nature of the injury and its impact on a particular client. Sometimes, the plaintiff can be personally used to bring the case to life, particularly with insurance adjustors. Indeed, many personal injury lawyers regard the plaintiff as a "lawyer's best piece of demonstrative evidence." By having the client present at a conference, the other negotiator can personally view the extent of the visible injuries and their effects. It also allows the other negotiator to become personally familiar with the plaintiff. Obviously, a client must be prepared for such a conference and the presentation itself must be planned. It also gives the plaintiff some valuable experience by having to react to meeting the other side of the lawsuit.

D. COMMUNICATION, INFORMATION EXCHANGE DURING NEGOTIATING SESSIONS, AND TACTICS

Negotiation depends on interpersonal communication. Without it, a negotiation would be no more than bidding or a simple exchange of offers. One of the important tasks of an effective legal negotiator is to communicate information to the other side. In an adversarial negotiation, Professor Williams suggests that the purpose of communicating this information is, in part, to cause the other side to feel and believe that (1) the negotiator has extraordinarily high expectations in this case, (2) the negotiator can credibly back up these expectations with the possibility a high outcome might be achieved, (3) the other side will have to make substantial concessions if it is going to settle the case, and (4) its best interest will be served by making those concessions.

Another important task of effective legal negotiators is to acquire and assess information from the other side. This ability directly depends on communication skills. By being skillful at reading their opponent's cues, they are able to acquire the necessary information about their opponent's needs, positions, and fears. As previously noted, Professor Williams found that effective legal negotiators are reasonable, analytical, realistic, and rational. With the input they receive through communication with the opposing side, they are able to assess the strengths and weaknesses of the case and to make appropriate judgments. In a problem-solving context, they are able to assess the parties' needs and concerns and to communicate problem-solving solutions.

1. EFFECTS OF POOR COMMUNICATION

When an information exchange appears to be insufficient or distorted, researchers have found that negotiators often lack a sufficient basis for recognizing common interests. Furthermore, it is widely recognized that communication isolation imposes constraints on the development of cooperation and is likely to promote distrust. For example, behavior resulting from excessive caution in a negotiation may be misconstrued by the other negotiator—thus encouraging defensiveness, which in turn may be misconstrued as threatening behavior. This threatening behavior ironically then reinforces the earlier suspicions that stimulated the original caution.

2. CASUAL CONVERSATION IN NEGOTIATION

A negotiator can gain valuable information through casual conversation about the opposing party, the opposing negotiator's time deadlines, the opposing party's needs, and so forth. Casual conversation is also a useful means of establishing rapport and open communication. When attempting to get to know the opposing negotiator through casual conversation, however, it is widely recommended that a negotiator should carefully avoid discussing some subjects unrelated to the negotiation, such as religion, politics, food, dress, and other items of personal preference. Otherwise, a negotiator may unintentionally evoke a strong negative reaction and thus damage rapport and communication.

3. LISTENING

Good listening skills during a negotiating session are important to legal negotiators for several reasons. First, listening is a fundamental method of acquiring information. Second, listening is a key to recognizing the needs and interests of the opposing party. Third, listening enables a negotiator to hear a point of view, which is critical to evaluating the opponent's position.

Fourth, listening allows a negotiator to reflect upon, paraphrase, and clarify the opponent's position and arguments. This type of reflection, paraphrasing, and clarification is likely to cause the opponent to be more attentive to the content of the negotiator's own statements.

For many lawyers, listening is not easy. Indeed, it seems that many lawyers prefer to talk rather than to listen to someone else. Furthermore, listening is difficult because an average person speaks at about 125 words per minute, but normally a person listens at about 500 words per minute. This listening rate encourages a person to interrupt (which tends to cut information flow), to leap to conclusions, and to think of responses or retorts rather than fully concentrating on what is said.

Studies also indicate that many difficulties in negotiating arise from the negotiator's failure to listen to and understand their opponent's proposals or concerns. One good method for avoiding this difficulty is for negotiators to first repeat their understanding of the opponent's proposals or concerns. Repeating the opponent's position often reveals misperceptions and can help avoid further misunderstandings.

In listening to other negotiators, commentators suggest that negotiators should try to focus on the use of phrases regarded as significant. For instance, when a negotiator uses the expression "by the way" or "before I forget" to introduce a statement, what is next stated is often very significant—despite the apparent attempt to disguise the statement as a spontaneous thought. When a negotiator introduces a statement with the expression "to tell the truth," "honestly," or "frankly" or when the negotiator states something like "I have laid all of my cards on the table," it is likely that the negotiator is not being honest or frank.

Commentators also suggest that negotiators should listen for so-called "pivotal" words or phrases, such as "essentially," "probably," "basically," "for the most part," "mostly," "all in all," and "generally." These "pivotal" words and phrases, as well as others, can be used by opposing negotiators to obscure important information.

Furthermore, listening is a key element in recognizing legitimate emotional statements involving strong hostility, blame, or even rage. Active listening is a positive way to deal with those emotions. Handled properly, active listening does not amount to agreement. As pointed out on the videotape, "From 'No' to 'Yes': The Constructive Route to Agreement," active listening immediately makes the speaker less defensive, more ready to reciprocate, and calmer. It also allows the speaker to become more rational, to be more open minded, and to become more communicative. On the other hand, hearing a "yes, but . . ." or direct argument in response to a legitimate emotional statement makes speakers feel that they have not really been heard.

Assume that one negotiator angrily states, "You have been responsible for destroying our business." The other negotiator responds, "I can see that you feel you have been hurt. You feel we are responsible, and you are very upset with us. What do you feel would be a fair solution *that as a practical matter you believe we might be willing to accept?*" In this example provided by Richard Givens in *Advocacy: The Art of Pleading a Cause*, the negotiator has, in part, demonstrated by "active listening" respect for the other side. This example also demonstrates how acknowledging hostility can be turned into a bargaining advantage rather than a disadvantage. As Givens states, "[a]cknowledging hostility expressed in a negotiation, without [defensively] reacting to it, can be a sign of strength, depending on the circumstances: An ant bite does not affect a rhino."

4. PROTECTING INFORMATION

Several widely recognized "blocking techniques" can be used to avoid answering the opposing negotiator's questions. These techniques are most often used to protect sensitive information. All of the following techniques must be carefully considered in light of the obligation to be truthful and the legal limits on fraudulent conduct, discussed below. In any event, these techniques should be sparingly used—limited to situations in which it is necessary to protect truly sensitive information and to avoid a needless loss of credibility.

(1) One technique is simply to ignore the question and move to some other area. In their book, *Interviewing, Counseling, and Neogtiating: Skills for Effective Representation*, Bastress and Harbaugh suggest that it is best to move to a topic that is likely to have some real interest.

(2) Another technique is to declare the question "off limits" on the ground of attorney-client privilege or some other plausible reason.

(3) Another technique is to respond to the opponent's question with a question. Charles Craver in his continuing legal education course materials illustrates this approach with the following simple interchange: If the question asked is, "Are you authorized to pay $100,000?" the response might be, "Are you willing to accept $100,000?" Professor Jacker provides another example: If the question asked is, "What would you think of an offer of $20,000?" the response might be, "Is that an offer?" The response might be used to indicate possible interest but not necessarily agreement, "Is that cash or over a period of time?" In this way, the negotiator does not have to answer the question directly.

Bastress and Harbaugh point out that this approach can be effective because it not only evades the question but also seeks clarification or elaboration—a legitimate negotiating goal. To be most convincing, Bastress and Harbaugh recommend that a negotiator should plan at least one follow-up question in response to an opponent's question probing for sensitive information. This approach is likely to provide an effective diversion.

(4) Another widely recognized blocking technique is to "under-answer or over-answer" the question. This technique involves responding generally to a specific question or responding narrowly to a general question. For example, if a question is a complex one,

the negotiator could focus the answer narrowly on a beneficial aspect of the question.

(5) Closely related to under-answering or over-answering is "answering honestly but incompletely." A classic example of answering this way is illustrated by the story about the buyer who was negotiating to purchase a small piece of property with a nice lake on it. Thinking about how the lakefront property might be developed, the buyer asked the seller if there were any snakes in the water. The seller assured the buyer there were none, which was a truthful answer. A more complete answer would have been that "there were no snakes in the lake because the alligators had eaten them all."

(6) Another blocking technique is to answer a different question than the one asked. Bastress and Harbaugh suggest the following ways to create another question to answer.

First, the pending question can be reframed to avoid revealing sensitive information. According to Bastress and Harbaugh, tell-tale signs that such a response is occurring include such introductory phrases as "As I understand your question, you want to know . . . ." or "I'd be pleased to tell you about . . . ."

Second, the pending question can be ignored and a direct answer to a different question given. To be effective, Bastress and Harbaugh point out the answer must be to a question "in the same part of the ballpark" as the one asked. A good example of this latter technique is provided by Givens in *Advocacy: The Art of Pleading a Cause*. In the following exchange, assume that the sensitive information that is sought to be protected relates to where X got a large amount of cash:

"Q. I gather that X must have had a large amount of money in cash in order to be able to buy a car with $25,000 that he pulled from his billfold. Where do you think he got the money?"

"A. You know, I think the dealer who sold the car was pretty amazed by that too."

"Q. I would suppose that X must really be overflowing with cash for this to happen . . ."

"A. [interrupting] It would certainly look that way."

"Q. Getting back to X, he must feel pretty cocky with that much money in his pocket; I wonder whether he carries it all the time and where he gets it."

"A. X must have felt pretty good to be able to hand that money to the dealer."

Third, a question seeking sensitive information can sometimes be blocked by answering a question that was recently asked again. Bastress and Harbaugh suggest that this technique is particularly effective on opponents "who are distracted, fumbling around with papers, or making extensive notes."

5. COMMUNICATING OFFERS AND CONCESSIONS

In their book, *Interviewing, Counseling, and Neogtiating: Skills for Effective Representation*, Bastress and Harbaugh suggest three "rules" for communicating offers in an adversarial context. First, the negotiator communicating an adversarial offer should be *brief* (but complete) to reduce the other party's time to prepare a response and force the other negotiator to react instinctively.

Second, the negotiator communicating an adversarial offer should be *specific* and should avoid "weasel words" that indicate the negotiator is not completely committed to the offer. Bastress and Harbaugh indicate that this "leakage" is particularly likely to occur within three to five minutes after the offer has been made.

Third, the negotiator communicating an adversarial offer should *justify* it by giving reasons for the specific amount of the offer. This approach reinforces the appearance of the negotiator's "commitment" to the position and allows the negotiator to resist moving from it unless a legitimate reason is presented to undermine the negotiator's articulated justification. Bastress and Harbaugh point out that the negotiator making the offer later can present legitimate reasons to abandon the offer and move to another position on the bargaining continuum for tactical reasons. These same considerations apply when concessions are made.

Particularly when figures are used, making offers is a notorious time for "slips of the tongue." The typical slip arises when a negotiator knows, for example, that $45,000 can be offered, but the negotiator first wants to say $40,000. If $45,000 slips out, no matter how quickly the negotiator retracts the inadvertent slip and changes the amount to $40,000, the impression created by the higher figure lingers. As noted earlier, negotiators should pay special attention to how offers are stated and should be on special guard in stating amounts.

Patterns of offers may give clues to a settlement point. Consider the following example given by Harry Edwards and James White in their book, *The Lawyer as a Negotiator*. They pose a situation in which there is a negotiation concerning the rental price per square foot of space. You believe the opposing negotiator's client has set a specific limit below which the negotiator may not go. The sequence of offers during the three-hour session is $2.00, $1.50, $1.25, and $1.19. From this pattern, it is possible to speculate on what the next offer or minimum amount ("bottom line" or "resistance point") might be. What is most apparent from the pattern, however, is the impression that the negotiator is *nearing* that point. This conclusion is consistent with empirical research that generally finds the size of concessions decreases as the negotiation progresses. Of course, knowledge of this pattern creates the possibility of false signals being communicated by a series of offers.

6. NONVERBAL BEHAVIOR IN NEGOTIATING SESSIONS

Much information in a negotiation can be obtained by carefully observing nonverbal behavior, including "telltale" mannerisms and furtive expressions. For example, the effect of intimidating tactics can be gauged by close observation. A close study of the initial facial reaction to an offer or concession may reveal much more than the verbal response. Tension is shown by blushing, strained laughter, contraction of facial muscles, fidgeting, and other body movements and mannerisms. Special emphasis should be placed on eye contact, body posture, and gestures.

In legal negotiation, probably the most important nonverbal behavior in the United States is eye contact. Generally speaking, direct eye contact is a good means of conveying honesty, confidence, and directness. It also allows negotiators to observe fully the effect of their communication. On the other hand, avoiding direct eye contact suggests uncertainty, weakness, and deference. Watching the other negotiator's nonverbal reactions to proposals or offers may reveal important insights into the other party's interests or resistance point.

A negotiator should be especially careful in interpreting nonverbal (as well as verbal) signals when the negotiator is dealing with someone of a different culture. What may mean one thing in one culture could mean something completely different in another culture. This problem most often arises in international negotiations, but it can also arise in any context in which there is diversity.

A negotiator should be careful to take into account the possibility of the other party intentionally giving false nonverbal signals. Feigned anger, for example, is often accompanied by false nonverbal signals, such as pounding one's fist on the table. When faced with suspicious or surprising nonverbal signals, a prudent negotiator should engage in some "reality testing" as a safeguard.

E. REACTING TO OFFERS

Many commentators suggest that if an offer is inadequate, the reaction should be immediate. Professor Jacker suggests that if the offer is outrageous, the lawyer should say so with feeling—let the reaction be seen and felt. Delaying such a reaction or delivering it without feeling undermines the lawyer's credibility. This sharp reaction is an example of a "*flinch*" or "*wince*." This tactic is simply an overt reaction to something the other negotiator says. Most often this tactic is used immediately after an offer has been stated. It is used to indicate that what was said is unacceptable or rejected.

Closely related to the flinch or wince, is the "*squeeze*," "*krunch*," or "*vice*." The purpose is to get opposing negotiators to bid against themselves. A typical indicator or warning sign of this tactic is a statement to the effect, "Oh, your client will have to do better than that."

Commentators suggest that the best response is to ask, in effect, "How much better will my client have to do?" If the other side says "a lot better," you would respond "well, how much is a lot better?" The point is to avoid letting the tactic work by bidding against yourself.

Another tactic related to a statement of an offer is *silence*. It is well known that cultures and individuals have different "tolerances" for silence. When a person becomes uncomfortable with silence, there is a tendency for that person to "fill the void" by taking. If a negotiator remains silent after an offer has been made, the opposing negotiator may inadvertently improve the offer as part of breaking the silence.

"*Limited authority*" is also a possible reaction to an offer. Limited authority involves stating that the offer or proposal appears to be acceptable, but it will need to be reviewed and approved by someone else. When used as a tactic, it can be a variation of a "good guy/bad guy" tactic discussed in section A, above.

On the other hand, it indeed might be true that the offer or proposal must be reviewed. In such an instance, commentators recommend that you ask, "You will recommend this, won't you?" By getting the opposing negotiator to say "yes" to this question, the opposing negotiator reaches "closure" and is more likely to support the offer or proposal when it is presented for review and approval. However, if the opposing negotiator responds that they cannot recommend it, then you need to go back and continue to negotiate.

F. COMMUNICATING OFFERS TO THE CLIENT

The commentary accompanying Rule 1.4 of the ABA's *Model Rules* indicates that "a lawyer negotiating on behalf of a client should provide the client with facts relevant to the matter, inform the client of communications from another party and take other reasonable steps that permit the client to make a decision regarding a serious offer from another party." Similarly, the comment indicates that a "lawyer who receives from opposing counsel an offer of settlement in a civil controversy or a proffered plea bargain in a criminal case should promptly inform the client of its substance unless prior discussions with the client have left it clear that the proposal will be unacceptable." Furthermore, the comment states that "[e]ven when a client delegates authority to the lawyer, the client should be kept advised of the status of the matter."

Rule 3-510 of the California Rules of Professional Conduct requires prompt communication of "[a]ll terms and conditions of any [written or oral] offer made to the client in a criminal matter." In all other matters, "[a]ll amounts, terms, and conditions of any written offer of settlement made to the client" must be promptly communicated. The "client" is defined to include "a person who possesses the authority to accept an offer of settlement or plea, or, in a class action, all the named representatives of the class." Although Rule 3-510 is limited by its terms to *written* offers in noncriminal matters, the comment to Rule 3-510 notes that "significant" *oral* offers of settlement must be communicated under the general obligation of keeping clients reasonably informed about significant developments imposed by Rule 3-500.

In conveying notice of an offer, lawyers routinely formalize their recommendation for the record. For example, when rejection of an offer is encouraged, Hornwood and Hollingsworth in their book, *Systematic Settlements*, suggest the following approach be used in the letter notifying the client of the offer. After indicating that in the lawyer's opinion "the offer is wholly inadequate," the letter states that "it is my duty to report to you all settlement offers. I would like to make it crystal clear that this letter in no way indicates our approval of this offer. I would strongly suggest at this time that the offer be rejected and that we proceed immediately to suit." On the other hand, it is important for a client to understand that litigation is not certain and that a time may come when taking what is certain (a settlement offer) may be best. Clients should be counseled about the advantages of settlement and should be told that statistically most cases are eventually settled rather than tried in court. Obviously, the degree and type of counseling depends on the lawyer-client counseling relationship that has developed.

According to the commentary accompanying Rule 1.4 of the ABA's *Model Rules*, the adequacy of the required communication depends on the kind of advice or assistance involved. As an illustration, the comment indicates that when time to explain a proposal exists, all important provisions of a settlement proposal should be explained to the client before proceeding to an agreement. The comment does point out, however, that "a lawyer ordinarily cannot be expected to describe trial or negotiation strategy in detail." The comment concludes that the guiding principle ought to be "that the lawyer should fulfill reasonable client expectations for information consistent with the duty to act in the client's best interests, and the client's overall requirements as to the character of representation."

Perhaps the most serious problem is the failure of lawyers to keep their clients informed about changing views of valuation. If clients are "left out" of this evolutionary process, they may naturally resist a settlement offer based on case developments and changing evaluations they have no knowledge of. Thus, client expectations created at the outset of the lawsuit may be a barrier to settlement, unless the client is kept informed and involved in a collaborative way.

G. TRUTH IN LEGAL NEGOTIATIONS

Lawyers routinely face issues of truthfulness (and partial truthfulness) in legal negotiation. In an adversarial negotiation, an important aspect of appearing to be tough is not letting oneself be duped or fooled. Professor Williams found that some cooperatives have a tendency to believe what is asserted at face value—particularly if they are under stress. Professor Williams points out that opponents may be trying to characterize the case in a light favorable to their side. They will not always be discussing the case in an objective, fair manner.

These situations raise a variety of issues. To what extent can you rely on the law and professional ethical standards to force opposing lawyers to make truthful statements? To what extent are you legally and ethically allowed to play on the ignorance or gullibility of opposing parties and their counsel to obtain an advantage for your client? To what extent can you conceal adverse facts or law? To what extent can you lie about your client's intentions or the value that your client places on certain aspects of the transaction? To what extent may you lie about your instructions?

The discussion below, subsequent sections in this chapter, and material in Chapter 5 address the general situations posed in Self-Test 4 in Chapter 1(G). Some norms from the diplomatic and business world are widely recognized. For example, in his book, *Give and Take: The Complete Guide to Negotiating Strategies and Tactics*, Chester L. Karrass states that "bluffing is part of negotiating[, but] the rules [in the business world] forbid and should penalize outright lying, false claims, bribing an opponent, stealing secrets through electronic devices, or threatening the physical well-being of the opponents or their families." In addition to business and diplomatic norms, lawyers must also take into account professional and legal requirements.

1. PROFESSIONAL AND LEGAL SAFEGUARDS AGAINST DISHONESTY IN LEGAL NEGOTIATIONS

Disciplinary Rule 7-102(A)(5) of the ABA's *Model Code* states that a lawyer shall not "[k]nowingly make a false statement of law or fact." In a similar vein, Disciplinary Rule 7-102(A)(7) provides that lawyers shall not "[c]ounsel or assist" their clients in conduct that lawyers know to be "illegal or fraudulent." Rule 8.4(c) of the ABA's *Model Rules* takes the same position: "It is professional misconduct for a lawyer to . . . engage in conduct involving dishonesty, fraud, deceit or misrepresentation." Model Rule 1.2(d) states that "[a] lawyer shall not counsel a client to engage, or assist a client, in conduct that the lawyer knows is criminal or fraudulent . . . ." Furthermore, Model Rule 4.1(a) provides that "[i]n the course of representing a client a lawyer shall not knowingly . . . make a false statement of material fact or law to a third person." Subpart (b) of Model Rule 4.1 imposes an affirmative duty "to disclose a material fact to a third person when disclosure is necessary to avoid assisting a criminal or fraudulent act by a client" *unless* this disclosure is prohibited by Model Rule 1.6, which prohibits disclosure of confidential information.

The questions of candor by lawyers who negotiate were hotly debated in formulating the above *Model Rules*. Because of floor amendments, the final version confusingly intertwines the obligation to disclose with restrictions resulting from the protection of confidentiality in Model Rules 1.6, 4.1(b), and 8.4(c) (confidentiality of information and truthfulness in statements to others). The prevailing view among many commentators is that the rules of professional ethics do little to regulate lawyer behavior other than to provide an additional sanction—lawyer discipline—for violating criminal, tort, and contract law.

The crime of false pretenses and others (such as theft by deception) impose criminal responsibility for certain types of false representations. Similarly, § 525 of the *Restatement (Second) of Torts* prohibits intentional fraudulent misrepresentations of fact, opinion, intention, or law. Pecuniary loss, reasonable reliance, and intent to induce that reliance are also elements that must be satisfied to create liability. Section

552(c) of the *Restatement* also provides liability for unintentional misrepresentations in a sale, rental, or exchange bargain, but limits damages to the difference in the value of what was parted with and the value of what was received. Under contract law, as recognized in § 164 of the *Restatement (Second) of Contracts*, relief may be obtained if an intentional or unintentional misrepresentation is either fraudulent or material.

The principal difficulty that lawyers face in dealing with affirmative untruths and misleading statements is separating nonactionable puffing from actionable misrepresentations. In the context of sales, the law recognizes that a certain degree of loose general sales talk should be permitted. Such puffing is considered to be offered as an expression of the seller's opinion—to be discounted as such by the buyer and on which no reasonable person would rely. Thus, under some circumstances, lawyers in negotiating a transaction may express certain suspect statements with respect to estimates, predictions, and client intentions within this puffing "privilege."

In a settlement context, some degree of loose, selective, or distorted manipulation of the "facts" by lawyers has been permitted as permissible puffing. Such manipulation often occurs in a discussion of the strengths and weaknesses of clients' legal positions. Sometimes, such an approach is termed "putting the facts in the most favorable light." Sometimes, too, it is accomplished by hypothetical statements ("What would you say if I told you that . . . ?").

It is also widely accepted that absolute honesty is not the prevailing norm when statements about a negotiator's authority to settle, a client's true interests, or a client's "bottom line" are involved. For example, in asserting demands, negotiators might flatly state that their clients will not settle for anything less than a certain figure; yet, in truth, their clients would quite readily accept a much lower amount. Such an approach is justified on the ground that the negotiator is not misrepresenting "a fact" in controversy.

In conclusion, the law and professional ethical standards will protect against only blatant misdeeds. Enough gray areas exist that great caution should be used in relying on the assertions made by others in legal negotiation. Blind reliance leads to dissatisfied clients, subsequent complex applications of substantive legal rules, and potential problems of proof that are best avoided. On the other hand, going too far in making or implying false or misleading statements creates the risk that a negotiator's own credibility will be undermined.

2. SPECIAL DUTIES IMPOSED ON FIDUCIARIES, INSURERS, PROSECUTORS, AND OTHERS

Special duties may be imposed on fiduciaries, insurers, prosecutors, and others in conducting legal negotiations. For example, as noted in Chapter 1(D), labor and management have a duty to bargain in good faith. Furthermore, when the parties stand in a fiduciary relationship, such as principal-agent or trustee-beneficiary, a duty of good faith and full and fair disclosure of all material facts may be recognized. This duty has been extended to certain types of contracts, such as suretyship, insurance, partnership, and joint venture. The Federal Truth in Lending Act requires creditors to make "meaningful disclosure" in consumer credit negotiations.

Some states have imposed on insurers the duty to bargain in good faith in an effort to reach a settlement. Section 790.03(h) of the *California Insurance Code*, for instance, condemns a wide variety of unfair claims settlement practices and provides for the recovery of punitive damages. In *Chodos v. Insurance Co. of North America* (1981), for example, a $200,000 punitive award for violating § 790.03(h) was held to be not excessive. Thus, the fear of punitive damages may encourage more ethical dealing. Another inducement is the risk of liability for damages beyond the policy limits when the insurer violates its duty to its own insured and refuses in bad faith to settle within the policy limits.

Disciplinary Rule 7-103(A) and (B) of the ABA's *Model Code* and Rule 3.8 of the ABA's *Model Rules* impose some restrictions on the conduct of prosecutors that may provide some protection to the defense in negotiations with prosecutors. The thrust of these restrictions is stated in Rule 3.8 of the ABA's *Model Rules*, which requires prosecutors in criminal cases to refrain from "prosecuting a charge that the prosecutor knows is not supported by probable cause," and to disclose in a timely manner to the defense all evidence or information "that tends to negate the guilt of the accused or mitigates the offense."

3. STRETCHING THE FACTS OF THE CASE

Professor Williams found that one of the common characteristics of effective negotiators is that they are seen as ethical, trustworthy, and honest. Effective negotiators must avoid being seen as liars, dishonest, and unethical—persons who cannot be trusted. As noted previously, conceptualizing the case in its most favorable light and defending that conceptualization are important means of establishing a strong negotiating position in an adversarial context. The outside limit on a negotiator's strategic conceptualization of the case, however, is the truth. If negotiators go too far, they will appear irrational, lose their credibility, and appear to be unethical. In this same vein, a common characteristic of effective negotiators is that they are reasonable, realistic, rational, and analytical. To be safe, Fisher and Ury suggest that a negotiator should make it a habit to always double-check the facts.

4. BLUFFS

Closely related to stretching the facts too far is bluffing. Bluffs are "designed to trick the opposing negotiators by distorting reality and promoting illusion." Bluffs often involve feigning weakness (*e.g.*, falsely asserting that there is nothing more that the client can do to reach agreement" or pretending the client has extra strength or resources (*e.g.*, falsely asserting that "my client doesn't need your client to make this deal go forward because my client has ample resources, if necessary, to go ahead alone"). In addition, bluffing can involve making threats that the bluffer knows will never be carried out (*e.g.*, falsely asserting that the client will buy from someone else if the client's terms are not met).

If a negotiator gets caught in a bluff, the negotiator will appear to be conniving and devious. Furthermore, if it is a factual bluff, the negotiator will appear to be a liar. According to Professor Williams, all of these impressions are best avoided by not engaging in bluffs.

In addition to impairing one's credibility if the bluffer has to back down, James C. Freund in *Smart Negotiating: How to Make Good Deals in the Real World* points out another risk with bluffing. It may turn out that the opposing negotiator *believes* the bluff, but the opposing side is unwilling to meet the demand. In such a case, the opposing side may simply decide to pursue another option without giving the bluffer the chance to modify the bluff. As a classic illustration of this risk, Freund gives the example of a buyer who bluffs on the buyer's "top price" for a piece of property—"only to wake up the next day with the property having been sold to a third party at a somewhat higher price [that] the bluffer would have been willing to pay." Thus, Freund aptly concludes, "[i]t's the fear of *succeeding* with the bluff but then having it blow up in your face that makes . . . the risks of bluffing generally unacceptable."

5. MAINTAINING A REPUTATION FOR BEING ETHICAL AND TRUSTWORTHY

Just as one's reputation for effectiveness (or ineffectiveness) will often precede a negotiator, a reputation for honesty, trustworthiness, and integrity will also precede a negotiator. Even though the clients in a negotiation may never have dealings with each other again, lawyers will often have to deal with persons who have contact with opposing counsel or with opposing counsel themselves.

H. INTIMIDATION

To deal with manipulation and the range of other intimidating competitive tactics, a negotiator must be attentive to the negotiation process. A negotiator must constantly consider (1) the opponent's strategy and style and (2) what the opponent is doing or attempting to do. As discussed previously, Professor Williams found that one of the common characteristics of effective negotiators is perception (skill in reading the opponent's cues). Another is self-control (not getting carried away with an emotional reaction).

The underlying dynamic of the competitive style is to move psychologically against the other person through words or actions. In an adversarial setting, the tactics include high demands, few concessions, exaggeration, ridicule, threat, toughness, and accusation to create pressure on the opponent. In essence, it is a manipulative approach designed to intimidate the opponent into accepting the competitive lawyer's demands.

If the competitive style is used effectively in an adversarial setting, competitive tactics will cause the opposing negotiators to lose confidence in themselves and their cases, to reduce their expectations of what they will be able to obtain, and to accept less than they otherwise would as a settlement outcome. The effects of this toughness on the opposing party's perceptions are crucial to the success of the competitive style. If too much pressure is applied, however, the negotiation will fail and an impasse will occur—losing the benefits of settlement. According to some commentators, a warning sign that a shift to competitive tactics is occurring may be the change to formal address (Mr./Mrs./Ms.) when first names have been used. This change in address may consciously or unconsciously help the negotiator depersonalize the bargaining interaction in a way that facilitates aggression.

To deal with competitive tactics, a negotiator must first recognize what is intimidating, manipulating, bullying, or cajoling. Intimidation includes statements attacking a negotiator or the opposing party. Such intimidation consists of derogatory remarks, statements containing manipulative connotations, or assertions of moral turpitude or fault. Effective competitive negotiators who use intimidation are careful to phrase the intimidating remarks in such a way that they are directed at the opposing lawyer's client, not the opposing lawyer. In this way, the negotiator avoids directly attacking the opposing lawyer's ego and face.

One immediate effect of using intimidation (which creates tension, mistrust, and hostility) is to distort the communication between the parties. It has been found that when people communicate under conditions of distrust and tension, they tend to overstate the extent of agreement and to overstate the extent of disagreement. Furthermore, in the areas of overstatement concerning agreement, competitive negotiators are led to believe that their opponents are closer to agreement than is, in fact, the case.

At the first sign of one of these tactics, Professor Williams suggests that a negotiator must respond. One way to respond is to make an immediate, devastating retort. The negotiator counters the aggressive tactic with refutation and counterargument. If such a retort does not occur to the negotiator, however, Professor Williams suggests another way to challenge the tactic: simply repeat back the intimidating, manipulating, bullying, or cajoling statement in question form. Repeating back the words or idea exposes the attack as silly, childish, and irrational. Confronting the attacker with the ridiculousness of the statement also shifts the burden of explanation back to the attacker to defend the statement, retract it, or replace it with a more reasonable one.

In sum, the basic defense against intimidation suggested by Professor Williams is to recognize the attack and to respond to it by either: (1) immediately voicing a come-back or (2) immediately repeating back to your opponent (verbatim or paraphrased) the words or idea just spoken in a question form. This approach demonstrates that intimidation will not work. In any event, the negotiator will have shown that the negotiator's defense is strong.

There are several other defenses against intimidating tactics that will assist a negotiator personally. One is a positive self-image. High commitment to the negotiator's goals also helps. Still another is limited authority. When a negotiator's authority is limited by the client, changes in position that the opposing negotiator hopes to extract by intimidation are necessarily also limited. Another possibility suggested by Fisher and Ury is to "sidestep" the attack, using silence to indicate unwillingness to accept unreasonable behavior, and then redirect the attack at the problem being negotiated.

Professor Williams has pointed out that female lawyers in legal negotiations sometimes experience comments from male lawyers that are derogatory or have manipulative connotations relating to the female lawyer's sex. A large amount of empirical research outside the legal profession has been conducted concerning the influence of the sex of the negotiator both on performance and the other negotiator's behavior. These studies have resulted in an assortment of contradictory findings.

According to Professor Williams, it seems predictable that lawyers who use competitive negotiating style would use some form of intimidation regardless of the sex of the opposing lawyer. Because competitive negotiators emphasize differences between themselves and their opponents and sex is an obvious and emotionally laden difference, sex provides an additional topic on which the attacks can be based. Thus, Professor Williams concludes that the kinds of intimidating statements reported by female lawyers are not caused or encouraged solely because they are female. This intimidation should be handled like any other form.

Empirical research outside the legal profession also suggests that negotiators tend to bargain more cooperatively with opponents of the same race rather than opponents of another race. Like sex, racial differences can be used as bases for intimidation. A joke or some ordinarily innocent statement may be taken personally by a negotiator of a different race or ethnic group and could unnecessarily create strained relations.

Age differences may influence negotiation and provide a basis for intimidation. In a legal context, age differences may be connected with positions of authority, experience, and expertise. For example, some lawyers may feel uncomfortable negotiating with persons of superior renown and expertise gained over a long period of time. Generally, these differences can be overcome by thorough preparation and by keeping in mind that both lawyers have a job to do for their respective clients. These differences do not, however, require that special deference beyond normal courtesies be given to experienced negotiators.

I. FACE SAVING

A largely unconscious process occurring during negotiations is face saving. There are great dangers when a negotiator is attacked in this way. Face saving is based on the need to appear capable and strong whenever possible and to avoid situations that make a person look foolish before others. Face saving is thus heavily dependent on the opposing negotiator's supposed status, prestige, and recognition in the eyes of others. It is a powerful factor that can have significant influence on legal negotiations and future relations of the negotiators.

Negotiation research suggests that when face-saving factors are involved, they are likely to arouse motives and induce behavior that is designed to prevent or repair damage to the negotiator's honor, self-esteem, reputation, status, and appearance of strength. These factors also significantly complicate the negotiation of tangible issues. Indeed, negotiators will often take highly costly steps to save face.

Researchers have found that opposition in a legal negotiation comes essentially in two forms: (1) idea opponents and (2) visceral opponents. Idea opponents disagree with the opposing negotiator on a particular issue or alternative. The difference is regarded as a matter of opinion. An idea opponent thinks the value is X; the other negotiator thinks the value is Y. Idea opponents can be addressed on an intellectual level with factual information. This situation presents the best opportunities for creative solutions. Integrative bargaining or problem solving may allow the negotiators to reach a solution in light of each side's interests, needs, concerns, and constraints.

On the other hand, visceral opponents are emotional adversaries who dislike the other negotiator's position, the other negotiator's point of view, and the other negotiator. Visceral opponents often attribute sinister motives to opposing negotiators, make accusations, and keep score. They do not respond to logic, facts, ideas, and evidence. *Once you create a visceral opponent, it is difficult to change the situation.* Thus, in the course of the negotiation, it is often recommended that a negotiator should be especially careful not to create such an opponent prior to agreement.

Attacking "face" is one of the principal ways of creating visceral opponents, especially when the opponent loses face in public. It evokes strong emotion and kindles retaliation. Furthermore, future dealings with the negotiator will be strained. Thus, in addition to not embarrassing, ridiculing, or humiliating the opposing negotiator (particularly in public), it has been suggested that a negotiator should exercise self-control: "Don't fight fire with fire. Don't take things too personally. Avoid judging the actions and motives of others."

J. TRANSFERENCE FACTORS

Until a person really knows the opposing negotiator, people tend to operate on certain assumptions. People often make these assumptions based on their past experiences and their own personality. In effect, people "transfer" past attitudes and feelings onto new people they meet. When those attitudes and feelings are powerful and largely unconscious, irrational conduct and serious errors of judgment may result.

For example, one indication that irrational transference factors are operating is an unreasonable dislike for the opposing negotiator. Likewise, irrational transference factors may be operating when there is an over-emotional response to tactics or positions of the opposing negotiator. Excessive attraction or admiration for the opposing negotiator may be another indicator. Another example is an excessive dread of negotiation and anxiety that far outweighs the objective anxiety appropriate to the negotiation.

Recognizing transference factors operating within oneself is the first step to dealing with them. In this way, a negotiator may become more tolerant of the reactions, allowing the negotiator to modify or resolve them in a satisfactory way.

K. THREATS AND PROMISES

A threat is technically the communication of an intent to punish the other side if the other side fails to concede. One function of a threat is to alter the other side's expected loss in the event the parties do not reach an agreement. Examples of typical threats include the threat to file suit, the threat to break off negotiations and make a deal with someone else, the threat to take a case to trial (with the attendant uncertainties and risks), and the threat of a work stoppage if the demand is not met. Effective threats should increase the likelihood of immediate compliance and concession making by the opposing party. Threats also can convey information about the threatener's true (or feigned) preferences and intentions. On the other hand, the use of threats tends to elicit hostility toward the conveyer of the threat.

Threats made by lawyers in legal negotiations are, of course, a form of coercion that can effectively persuade.

1. LEGAL SAFEGUARDS AGAINST IMPERMISSIBLE THREATS

The difficulty legal negotiators face is that the law views certain kinds of threats as permissible while others are not. At one extreme are those threats that are clearly permissible, such as threats made in good faith by lawyers to the effect that a civil action will be commenced unless their clients' legitimate claims are satisfied. At the other extreme are those threats that violate criminal extortion statutes. Such statutes, for example, would typically cover threats, conveyed from clients through their lawyers, to physically injure opposing parties or their property in the future unless money is paid to satisfy a claim.

Likewise, typical criminal extortion statutes would cover threats made by lawyers in the course of legal negotiation to accuse opposing parties of crimes unrelated to the subject of the negotiation. Such threats are condemned because they represent a potentially oppressive use of the criminal law to defeat just claims or defenses in civil litigation and because of the resulting silence if the threat is successful. Furthermore, under typical statutes, it is unlawful to threaten to file a formal complaint or to threaten to publicize the fact that a crime has been committed. Most statutes also cover threats to expose some disgraceful defect or secret that, if publicized, would result in the victim's public ridicule or disgrace. Of course, it is no defense that the victim is, in fact, guilty of the crime or possesses the defect that was threatened to be exposed.

The most uncertain area under the criminal extortion statutes is how far lawyers may go in threatening to expose the opposing parties' guilt unless reasonable restitution is made for harm done. Provided no more than damages for the harm done is demanded, some courts hold that the required "intent to extort or gain" is lacking. Some statutes also provide a specific defense under these circumstances. For example, § 135.75 of the New York Penal Law protects from liability a "defendant [who] reasonably believed the threatened charge to be true and . . . [whose] sole purpose was to compel or induce the victim to take reasonable action to make good the wrong which was the subject of [the] threatened charge."

When dealing with statutes that do not specifically require an intent to gain, however, other courts have found the threatener guilty. Indeed, the weight of authority rejects the defense that the threatener believed that the money or property was owed and that the debtor was guilty of the crime for which exposure was threatened. Obviously, the applicable law must be checked before using such threats.

In addition to the possible application of criminal extortion statutes to threats, lawyers must concern themselves with Disciplinary Rule 7-105(A) of the ABA's *Model Code*. This rule states that lawyers "shall not present, participate in presenting, or threaten to present criminal charges solely to obtain an advantage in a civil matter." A few jurisdictions have extended this prohibition to administrative or disciplinary charges. Disciplinary Rule 7-105(A) has also been applied to veiled allusions to the criminal nature of a person's conduct. In addition, courts have treated Disciplinary Rule 7-105(A) as a pure attempt prohibition—requiring only the showing of the threat even though no criminal charges were brought or any settlement achieved.

The greatest ambiguity in Disciplinary Rule 7-105(A) concerns the qualifier "solely." Is that provision violated if lawyers have a "mixed" motivation? Several decisions have found a violation even though a lawyer was motivated by concerns in addition to obtaining an advantage in civil litigation. Other decisions, in effect, have read this qualifier strictly and have limited the application of this provision to ill-founded criminal charges. For example, in *In re Decato* (1977), the New Hampshire Supreme Court held that, absent a demand for payment, a threat to file a well-founded criminal charge was not made merely to obtain an advantage in a civil action and was therefore permissible.

On the civil side, threats to invoke the criminal process may be actionable as a tort, such as abuse of process. Similarly, under sections 175 and 176(1)(b) of the *Restatement (Second) of Contracts*, if threats of criminal prosecution are made in the course of a contract negotiation, the contract may be voidable on grounds of duress. Section 176(1)(c) goes even further, however, and deems a bad faith threat to use civil process to be improper and thus voidable. Comment (d) to § 176 indicates that bad faith might consist of a belief that no reasonable basis for the threatened process existed, knowledge that the threat would involve a misuse of process, or a realization that the demand was exorbitant.

In § 176(2), the *Restatement (Second) of Contracts* also deems a threat to be improper "if the resulting exchange is not on fair terms" and any one of these three conditions are met: (1) "the threatened act would harm the recipient and would not significantly benefit the party making the threat"; (2) "the effectiveness of the threat in inducing the manifestation of assent is significantly increased by prior unfair dealing by the party making the threat"; or (3) "what is threatened is otherwise a use of power for illegitimate ends." The lesson to be learned from these *Restatement* provisions is that the courts will intervene in extreme cases. The key is a great difference in bargaining power. For example, in *Jamestown Farmers Elevator, Inc. v. General Mills, Inc.* (1977), the Eighth Circuit found improper duress in a threat to destroy small grain dealers by bringing regulatory actions to revoke the dealers' licenses unless grain was delivered to General Mills.

2. EFFECT OF THREATS ON THE NEGOTIATION

Negotiation studies indicate that threats are most likely to occur when (1) the threatener has no positive interest in the other person's welfare and (2) the threatener believes the opponent has no interest in the threatener's welfare. When these conditions are met, the threat is likely to be effective, or at least to do no harm to the threatener's position.

Negotiation studies also indicate that agreement is most easily reached when no threats are made by either side. Agreement is more difficult to reach when a threat is made by one of the negotiators. Agreement is extremely difficult or impossible when threats are made by both negotiators. Just as with toughness, use of threats greatly increases the likelihood of impasse.

3. COMMUNICATING THREATS AND PROMISES

A threat (a commitment to take action) should be distinguished from a warning (a prediction of adverse action if a concession is not made). Thus, threatening behavior can be softened by calling it a warning. This characterization tends to relieve the other side of the perceived need to counterthreaten to defend its prestige. Indeed, effective negotiators often take care to say, with each threat, that it was not a threat.

Promises and threats are interrelated in this sense: the flip side of an effective promise is the implied failure to reward the other side. One general problem of making promises, however, is that if they are too large, they may be regarded as bribes. On the other hand, the use of credible promises tends to elicit a positive regard for the conveyer of the promise.

Underlying the effectiveness of both threats and promises is a negotiator's credibility of commitment to future promised or threatened behavior. Obviously, actual past fulfilled commitments (both promises and threats) are critically important to credibility. If the client or the negotiator has been caught lying, bluffing, or cheating on past commitments, the threat of future action is diminished.

L. CONFLICT ESCALATION AND ENTRAPMENT

Threats and counterthreats and hard bargaining by both sides encourage what is known as "conflict escalation and entrapment." According to Pruitt and Rubin, a rising level of conflict causes the negotiators to develop negative attitudes and perceptions and stimulates the desire to defeat or outmaneuver the other side. The willingness to communicate or even to make small concessions is reduced. The negotiators also begin to see the other side as a member of a category rather than an individual.

"Entrapment" is regarded as a special form of conflict escalation. When the parties become committed to certain goals, they can become irrational in terms of the amount of time and resources that they will commit to achieving the goals. A classic example of entrapment is a "bidding war" at auctions in which bidders continue to bid against each other to unrealistic levels. Pruitt and Rubin explain that entrapment can occur when the parties believe that the goal is "just ahead."

Parties may also become entrapped when they feel that they have invested so much that it is now too costly to give up. Face saving can also be a factor in light of this investment. As Charles Craver aptly points out in his book, *Effective Negotiation and Settlement*, negotiators "should never continue negotiations merely because of the substantial amount of time and resources they may have already expended in an unsuccessful attempt to obtain mutually acceptable terms. This is particularly true when they are tempted to extend present interactions for the purpose of punishing their recalcitrant opponents."

To avoid entrapment, Pruitt and Rubin suggest setting limits prior to the negotiation. Careful assessment of costs and periodic review of them is another safeguard against entrapment. Bastress and Harbaugh suggest that a concession is another means of breaking out of an entrapped negotiation.

M. NEGOTIATING BREAKS AND RESTARTING STALLED NEGOTIATIONS

Professor Gifford points out that breaks, recesses, and breakdowns should be expected as a normal part of the dynamic and cyclical negotiation process. Breaks, recesses, and breakdowns may be used for both offensive and defensive purposes. On the offensive side, breakdowns may occur as negotiating ploys designed to put pressure on the opponent. For example, negotiators may "walk out" of negotiation sessions—or threaten to do so—with the hope that the other side will make concessions to avoid a deadlock. On the defensive side, Professor Gifford notes that a negotiator may call a negotiating break when (1) the emotional climate has shifted against the client; (2) new or unexpected information or positions arise; (3) the negotiator's own tactics are not having the effect anticipated; or (4) the negotiator is tired or confused.

Professor Jacker suggests that as part of the close of a negotiating session, the next meeting time should be established. If a specific time is not established, the second best approach is to establish the method for determining the time. If neither of these approaches are used at the end of the session, a face-saving technique for both sides may be needed to get the negotiations restarted. For example, new information or the suggestion of a third party such as a judge could be cited as grounds for restarting stalled negotiations. Another means might be to suggest that a mediator be brought in to help get the negotiations moving. Even this suggestion, however, might be viewed as a sign of weakness.

Otherwise, proposing the reopening of negotiations may result in what is commonly termed as a "loss of image." As Professor Gifford points out, the basic problem is the perception that "the lawyer's willingness to continue negotiation, without a change in circumstances, often suggests that [the negotiator's] earlier 'toughness' was mere bluffing and [thus the negotiator] can be pressured into further concessions."

Proposing the reopening of negotiations also creates the possibility of being branded as having a "weak case" or a "weak negotiating position." This characterization is a variant of what Professor Williams calls the "oldest trick in the book." Professor Williams recommends that this intimidating tactic be handled directly. A negotiator faced with this situation should state that both lawyers know that they have an obligation to their respective clients to try to reach a satisfactory settlement and that it is in the best interest of both parties to reach a negotiated settlement. Givens suggests another possible approach. It may be possible to recast the beginning of negotiations as a sign of *strength*, as illustrated by the following two examples: "We are raising the subject of settlement because we know you can't do so [with] the circumstances favoring us as they do, since it might appear a sign of weakness for you to do so" or "We are raising the subject of settlement because our position is strong enough that we are not concerned about this being interpreted as a sign of weakness."

N. DEALING WITH IRRITATING, INEFFECTIVE, COMPETITIVE NEGOTIATORS

Professor Williams suggests that every effort should be made to avoid letting personality seriously interfere with the conduct of a case. Nonetheless, personality is a factor, and in some instances it may decisively preclude rational settlement discussions. Indeed, Professor Williams' empirical research has shown that a certain segment of the practicing bar are impossible opponents. As discussed previously, these lawyers are ineffective competitive lawyers. They are irritating, rigid, hostile, loud, quarrelsome, egotistical, headstrong, and arrogant. They act in this way because they are not prepared on the facts, not prepared on the law, and unsure of the value of the case—they use bluff and bluster as a substitute.

In dealing with this type of opponent, the hallmark of every effective negotiator is self-control. As previously stated, Professor Williams suggests that a negotiator should adopt the position of "no negotiation" with such opponents as long as the irritating tactics continue. Professor Williams maintains that the opponent's attempts to negotiate should not be acceded to and negotiations with such opponents should not be initiated. However, Professor Williams maintains that occasional, even frequent, contacts with the opponent are useful for two reasons. First, these contacts serve to educate an unprepared opponent about the case. Every conceivable excuse should be made to make brief, polite, informative telephone calls, to send copies of documents, and to send brief messages telling of developments. Second, these contacts help establish a nonthreatening atmosphere and invite cooperation.

In the course of these contacts, Professor Williams suggests that lots of empathy and free concessions should be given. As part of this pattern, it would be appropriate to promise to be willing to negotiate when the opponent is prepared and is ready to get down to serious negotiations. In the meantime, the litigation process should be kept actively moving, which indicates the lawyer is preparing for trial and forces the opposing lawyer to prepare. Remember that Professor Williams found that this type of opponent is not only ineffective as a negotiator but also is ineffective at trial.

In sum, Professor Williams recommends that a negotiator be patient and outwit this type of opponent. The result will be that the opponent will fold at the last minute before trial because the opponent fears trial even more than rational negotiation. The opponent will either accept a long-standing invitation to negotiate the case reasonably and rationally or will farm the case out to a litigator for trial. Either way, according to Professor Williams, the negotiator will have succeeded. The negotiator will have controlled the situation and will have forced the opponent's hand. The negotiator will either gain a favorable last-minute settlement or a chance to work with a new (and presumably more rational) lawyer to settle or try the case.

Richard Givens takes a similar position. Givens states that "only firmness will defeat bullying" and that "[i]t may be necessary to go to the brink to find out whether an agreement can be reached." Givens does suggest the alternative possibility of simply stating what is going on as a possible defense against bullying tactics of an impossible negotiator: "If I were in your position with the difficulties you are facing, I would probably yell very loud, pound the table, and take an extreme position too, so I don't mind your doing that. Please go right ahead. We both know it has no bearing on the actual result we are going to have to reach." If the negotiator refuses to negotiate seriously and remains calm, "[t]he shouter may have very little adrenalin left by the end of the discussion and may even capitulate when the *real* bargaining takes place."

CHAPTER 5

REACHING AGREEMENT OR "FINAL BREAKDOWN," WRAPPING UP THE DETAILS, DRAFTING THE AGREEMENT, INTERPRETING THE SETTLEMENT, FAIRNESS, AND DEFECTS IN SETTLEMENTS

A. TIME PRESSURES AND DEADLINES

Time pressure is a perceived need to end the negotiation quickly. Time deadlines and pressures have significant effects on negotiation. Studies indicate that the less time pressure felt by negotiators, the better they tend to do in a particular case. When both negotiators feel time pressure, there is a greater probability that making concessions (adopting a cooperative approach) will be a profitable strategy. On the other hand, when time pressures are not felt, concession making is less likely to be profitable. Studies also indicate that when experimental negotiations were conducted in stages, increased time pressure lowered both negotiators' expectations, levels of demand, and their tendency to bluff at the first bargaining session.

Time pressures can be useful in the negotiation process. First, time pressures can create a sense of urgency and thus move the parties to act. Second, they tend to force the negotiators to reveal their true positions and cause parties to reassess the minimum terms upon which they would be willing to settle.

Time pressures have several sources. Sometimes, time pressure relates to the nature of the work week. For instance, many negotiations are concluded late on Friday afternoons or just before the start of holidays. In other instances, they are closely related to contract obligations. For example, a widely recognized aspect of collective bargaining between management and labor is the "eleventh hour" effect in which agreements are reached shortly before contract expiration. In lawsuit negotiation, the time pressure arises from the approach of trial—which is closely associated with Stage Three of legal negotiation (emergence and crisis). Insurance defense counsel sometimes use the trial deadline to pressure opponents by refusing to enter into serious negotiations until a few days (sometimes a few hours) before trial. Professor Williams suggests that they would be robbed of this tactic if plaintiffs' counsel adopted a firm policy of never negotiating once the case is within a week of trial. The effect would be to move the operative deadline to a week before trial. It might yield advantages to one or both sides.

Time limits may also be created unilaterally. For example, a negotiator may use an "option" approach in real estate or lawsuit negotiation—"This offer expires at 9:00 a.m. tomorrow morning." Even though this 9:00 a.m. deadline was of the negotiator's own making (and often is imaginary), the other side will frequently accept it as real.

Another way to create time pressure unilaterally is by making the other side believe that success is likely only at the expense of considerable time loss. This kind of time pressure can be conveyed by a willingness to drag out the negotiation by continually raising new issues, consulting with the client for instructions, and other similar tactics. Finally, time pressure can be unilaterally created by making the likelihood of breakdown seem imminent without agreement.

It is to a negotiator's advantage if unilaterally created time pressures seem to stem from some source other than the negotiator. For example, a negotiator who controls the negotiation schedule might encourage the negotiation session to continue into the night or into the weekend. This approach would put time pressure on an adversary with personal commitments (family or impending travel) or other obligations (an upcoming trial in another case) that do not affect the negotiator in the same way (an unmarried negotiator with no impending work obligations or travel plans).

When unilaterally created deadlines are announced, the opposing negotiator should carefully analyze the deadline. Is the deadline real or imaginary? Sometimes, insight on this question can be gained by determining what the opposing party has to gain by setting the deadline.

B. NARROWING THE DIFFERENCES AND CLOSURE TECHNIQUES

Several techniques can be used to narrow the differences between the parties and to bring a negotiation to an end.

1. "TRIAL BALLOONS"

A "trial balloon" is an excellent means of exploring possible combinations or rearrangements that might provide a basis for narrowing the differences or reaching closure. Trial balloons may open up new possibilities, provide information that might not otherwise be given, allow the parties to explore a better deal, and help the parties find common ground. Typically, trial balloons are introduced by questions that begin with "what if."

For example, In *Give and Take: The Compete Guide to Negotiating Strategies and Tactics*, Chester L. Karrass provides the following illustration of "what ifs" a buyer might use with a seller: "What if we double the order (or halve it)?" "What if we give you a one-year contract?" "What if we drop the warranty (or increase it)?" "What if we supply the material?" "What if we own the tooling?" "What if we buy [X] and [Y] instead of just [X]?" "What if we let you do the job during the slow season?" "What if we buy your total production?" "What if we supply technical assistance?" "What if we change the type of contract?" "What if we change the specifications like this?" "What if we give you progress payments?" etc. These types of trial balloons often reflect the interest-based, "pie-expanding" ideas discussed in Chapter 3(D).

According to Karrass, the counterpart of the "what if" is "would you consider?" This question could be used in response to probe an offer or a "what if." Karrass provides the following illustrations of such "would you consider" questions: "Would you consider taking [a different grade of] products, a larger delivery, spare parts, a change in specifications, . . . last year's model?" etc.

2. SPLITTING THE DIFFERENCE

Splitting the difference is a frequently used closure technique. This simple expedient is most appropriately used when the difference is a small one. However, it tends to be a trap when the difference between the parties' position is a large one. Many commentators suggest resistance in such a situation. For example, in *"In Business as in Life—You Don't Get What You Deserve, You Get What You Negotiate,"* Chester L. Karrass suggests the following response: "[My client] cannot afford to. [My client] needs 75% of the difference."

3. LOG-ROLLING

When the negotiation involves multiple issues, the negotiators may be able to bring closure by forming a package deal. In this way, the parties can make trade-offs resulting in a mutually satisfactory conclusion. This approach is called "log-rolling." Professor

Gifford points out that clients often find it difficult to decide on which issues they are willing to concede— these choices are made only after they know which issues the other side values the most. According to Professor Gifford, knowledge of these differing priorities helps explain why closure is reached in most cases. One of the principal means of taking advantage of these differing priorities is the log-rolling technique. The joint benefit is increased "beyond what would be accomplished if each party conceded an equivalent amount on each individual issue."

4. OBJECTIVE CRITERIA

In *Getting to Yes: Negotiating Agreement Without Giving In*, Fisher and Ury suggest using *objective criteria* as the preferred technique in resolving differences. They suggest that any standard or procedure may be used, provided it is regarded as legitimate and independent of the parties. As discussed in Chapter 3(D), above, examples of objective criteria or standards include market price of a good or service, replacement cost, scientific or professional standards, or standard industry customs or practices. Objective opinions of independent experts would perform the same function. When this technique is used to narrow the differences, Fisher and Ury recommend that the issue be cast in terms of a search for objective criteria, such as a "fair" price—recognizing that there may be several possible objective reference points.

5. FAIR PROCEDURES

Splitting the difference, discussed above, is an example of Fisher and Ury's objective (fair) procedures to bring closure. Other examples of such procedures include taking turns or flipping a coin. Another such procedure is for each side to submit a "final" offer to an independent decision maker, whose sole responsibility is to select between them. This latter approach is sometimes used to set wages or to fix prices during long-term supply contracts. In the example of the two sisters who both wanted the orange in Chapter 2(D)(2)*(a)*, if the two sisters agreed to divide the orange and each take half, a fair procedure would be for one sister to cut the orange and the other would then choose which half she wanted.

Fisher and Ury maintain that using fair procedures and objective criteria has several benefits. First, perceived fairness may increase the durability of the agreement. Second, the parties may find it easier to reach agreement when they agree to a standard rather than give in to the opposing party's position. Third, time and effort may be saved because it reduces arguments over positions, especially when multiple interests or parties are involved.

C. AGREEMENT OR "FINAL BREAKDOWN"

At some point, one or both of the negotiators will move to either close an agreement or reach an impasse or deadlock. This crisis stage (Stage Three) is usually triggered by the arrival of a deadline, such as trial or some other event. At the crisis stage, Professor Williams aptly notes that it is never a "yes" or "no" situation. There are three choices: (1) accepting the last offer; (2) rejecting the other side's last offer and going to trial; or (3) modifying the last offer enough to call it a new alternative. Professor Williams points out that the third choice is often the key to success and is the best way to save face at the moment of deadlock and continue negotiating.

In a litigation context, if the parties are unable to arrive at a settlement and the negotiations are not revived, a *"final breakdown"* has occurred and the case goes to trial for resolution. Commentators use this term because not all breakdowns in negotiation are really final. As noted previously, the negotiation process is often a cyclical process— with various starts and stops.

In a transactional setting, when negotiations end in a final breakdown and it is later discovered that the other side may have engaged in bad faith, Professor Robert Summers points out in his article, *"Good Faith" in General Contract Law and the Sale Provisions of the Uniform Commercial Code*, that the victim of bad faith at the negotiation stage cannot recover in contract because no contract was ever formed. Professor Summers, however, posits that two "negotiation" torts may be possible. First, a right of action in tort might be based on negotiating without serious intent to contract. Second, such a right of action might be based on withdrawing a negotiating proposal after foreseeably inducing the other side to rely on it.

D. FINALIZING THE AGREEMENT

If the parties agree to a settlement and enter Stage Four (as discussed in Chapter 2(F)), they will be concerned with the following phases: (1) working out the final details of the agreement; (2) justifying and reinforcing each other and the clients about the desirability of the agreement; and (3) formalizing the agreement.

1. WORKING OUT THE DETAILS

If the parties come to an agreement, the first step will be to work out details of the agreement. Some lawyers negotiate in a way that keeps the details alive and active in the ongoing discussion. This approach is a common feature of a problem-solving strategy and integrative bargaining, in which alternative solutions to each sub-issue are explored and creative solutions sought.

In contrast, lawyers following an adversarial approach prefer to negotiate only the most basic issues, such as money. They leave the other issues to be "wrapped up" after general agreement has been reached. Sometimes, other lawyers separate the issues according to how difficult they are to resolve, then resolve them working from the easiest to the most difficult. Whatever variation or combination is used, the lawyers at some point have an agreement, yet the important details may remain to be worked out.

a. The "Oh, by the Ways"

The details to be worked out are known as "*Oh, by the ways.*" These details must be considered important to the overall quality of the agreement. Indeed, the value of the settlement can change dramatically based on the details worked out by the negotiators after the basic agreement has been reached. In an adversarial setting, an effective negotiator may be able to take advantage of the other negotiator's "battle fatigue"—"the strong desire to get the whole thing over with." Furthermore, working out the details often provides opportunities for enhancing the benefits to both parties. Thus, the "details" should be given the attention they deserve.

b. "Nibbling"

"Nibbling" is more than working out the details. This tactic involves asking for a comparatively small benefit just at the close of the deal. According to Chester L. Karrass in his book, *Give and Take: The Complete Guide to Negotiating Strategies and Tactics*, nibbling works because most parties or negotiators are "impatient." They have psychologically "closed the deal" in their minds and want to move onto other matters. Furthermore, they want to be "liked[,] show how fair they are, and . . . build future relationships." Thus, they "are willing to make concessions to achieve these goals."

One defense against nibbling is to recognize nibbling and "resist the tendency to give in." Another defense is to ask for something in return. As John Patrick Dolan states in his videotape, *Negotiate Like the Pros*, a negotiator should ask the nibbler, in effect, "If I do that for you, what are you willing to do for me?" Requesting this kind of "trade-off" goes a long way toward discouraging nibbling.

c. *"Escalation"*

In this context, "escalation" involves unilateral changes in the agreement *after* the agreement has been reached and is legally binding. In effect, a new contract replaces the prior one if the escalation tactic works. In *Give and Take: The Compete Guide to Negotiating Strategies and Tactics*, Chester L. Karrass provides the following example of escalation. A seller advertises a car for sale at a certain price. In response to an advertisement, a potential buyer engages in an extensive negotiation. The seller reluctantly agrees to accept $700 less than the asking price. The buyer gives a $100 deposit. At this point, the parties have a legally binding agreement. The buyer then returns the next day with a certified check for $400 less than the full balance due. The buyer "cries a lot and explains that this is all that can be raised." Is the seller likely to "accept this deal or not"? Karrass suggests that "most people will."

Watch particularly for escalation in certain international contexts. It often works when one party to the transaction wants to maintain good relations with the escalating party, the weaker party lacks good alternatives, or the party is otherwise committed to the deal with the escalating party.

Karrass points that the first step to countering this type of escalation is "a better understanding of how and why it works." In addition, Karrass raises several options, such as (1) caucusing to gain time to think; (2) calling the other person's "bluff" (if that is what it is) and "giving strong consideration to walking away from the deal"; and (3) counterescalating. In the car example, above, having a large security deposit as earnest money would help prevent this tactic. To help prevent escalation, Karrass suggests that negotiators should try to have as many "high-level" persons sign the agreement. "The more names on the contract, the more difficult it is [for unethical people on the other side] to escalate." Furthermore, before the agreement is signed, you can ask the other party directly for assurances that escalation will not take place.

Karrass concludes that "[t]hese countermeasures are not foolproof." As Karrass states, "escalators [know] exactly what [they] are doing. [They have] decided deliberately that the odds of winning are good." In such a situation, Karrass recommends that the escalation should be tested "vigorously." Karrass concludes that "[y]ou may find that [the escalator] has more to lose than you do." Usually, "[t]he escalator is no fool [and] is just a tough gambler who does not deserve an easy victory."

2. JUSTIFYING AND REINFORCING THE AGREEMENT

Often, agreement appears to be reached when either one party or the other first arrives at its deadline or perceives that the other has made all the concessions it can be expected to make. Professor Williams has pointed out that once agreement has been reached, the psychology of the moment is that of "battle fatigue." Furthermore, just after an agreement of major proportions has been reached, there is a tendency to have second thoughts ("buyer's remorse"). Suddenly, the negotiators may feel that every other alternative looks better than the one chosen.

To keep these second thoughts from having damaging effects, Professor Williams urges that a negotiator should make the other side feel good about the agreement. Negotiators and mediators involved in the negotiation should help justify and reinforce the agreement (which, at the same time, helps remove the negotiator's own second thoughts). The negotiators should avoid any indication they think that they got the best of the other side ("You left a lot of money on the table" or "I didn't think I could steal so much money from you in this case"). In other words, the negotiator should not gloat.

In sum, once a solution is made, psychological reinforcement may be required by all involved. Effective negotiators will not only provide reinforcement for their own clients but will take great pains to provide adequate reinforcement to the opposing negotiator and party. Mediators can help rationalize compromises by pointing out that the parties are being wise, not weak, in making them. If this reinforcement is not provided, the negotiator may well be faced with a subsequent repudiation of the agreement by the disgruntled opponent.

3. FORMALIZING THE AGREEMENT

At some point in negotiation resulting in an agreement, documents formalizing that agreement will ordinarily need to be prepared. Those documents may include formal contracts, structured settlement agreements, releases, covenants not to sue, payment guarantees, deeds, letters of intent, or simply a written apology. Indeed, one of the parties may provide a proposed agreement at the outset or during the negotiation from which the negotiators work.

Whether a proposed agreement or other documents are used by the parties during the negotiation or are drafted by one of the parties after agreement on the principal items has been reached, the person who prepares the first working draft gains several significant advantages. First, the initial drafter controls the format of the agreement. Second, the initial drafter can select the boilerplate provisions and language favorable to the drafter's client. As one commentator has aptly noted, "[a]ll boilerplate is not the same." Third, the non-drafting party has the burden of proposing and justifying changes. In most instances, few changes will be insisted upon and the changes made will be insubstantial. Fourth, when the non-drafting party requests changes, the drafter may be able to trade that change for some other concession.

One way to become the initial drafter of the document is to take good notes and volunteer to prepare "a rough draft" of the agreement or other necessary documents. Another way is to present a proposed agreement at some point in the negotiation session. It is often to your advantage to present that agreement or some other document in a professionally *printed* format. Printed forms, such as contracts, purchase agreements, and leases, give the appearance of being less susceptible to change than the same document in less formal format. A printed form can be counteracted by preparing a rider covering the changes or by replacing it with a customized draft.

In preparing the draft, a negotiator must be cautious in relying on form books, especially in a transaction setting. Forms are often taken from previously negotiated documents, which may include compromises unfavorable to the negotiator's client. Forms also may inhibit your creativeness, but are especially useful in helping avoid omission of important points. As noted earlier, it is also useful to consult initial proposals (and the resulting final agreements) drafted by other negotiators who have been on the same side of the transaction or lawsuit. This approach will provide insight into what others in a similar position asked for initially.

4. "POST-SETTLEMENT SETTLEMENT"

Howard Raiffa has introduced the term "post-settlement settlement" to describe a procedure to see if the negotiated agreement can be improved. "Post-settlement settlement" involves the submission of the negotiated and binding final agreement to a third party for analysis. In this way, a final search for joint gains is made, but neither party is bound to accept the third party's recommendations. Assuming that the agreement is indeed enforceable, the parties' BATNA is the agreement that was submitted. Improvement in outcomes can be judged against the negotiated results. The principal drawback to this approach is that it requires mutual agreement to go through "post-settlement settlement"—which, of course, is a problem when one party regards this procedure as a waste of time and expense.

5. PROOF OF THE SETTLEMENT, CONSENT JUDGMENTS, AND DISMISSALS WITH PREJUDICE

In general, compromise agreements do not have to be in writing to be valid—unless (1) it is necessary to comply with the statute of frauds or (2) it is required by local court rules. In some jurisdictions, a writing may be required if the subject matter of the compromise falls within the statute of frauds. This statute, however, applies only to the subject matter of the compromise agreement and not to the antecedent claim. For example, a compromise agreement requiring one party to convey real estate to another would fall under the statute. On the other hand, the compromise of a dispute involving ownership of land, in which one party was required to pay money to the other without a transfer of land, would not fall under the statute of frauds. The subject matter of the compromise agreement is the agreement to pay money, not the conveyance of land.

In some jurisdictions, local rules and court procedures may also require a signed writing as evidence of the agreement. When writings are required, courts are likely to hold the parties strictly to the requirement. For example, in *Davies v. Canco Enterprises* (1977), a settlement agreement that had been incorporated into the transcript of a deposition but which had not been signed by either party was "of no force and effect."

It is good practice to make the agreement part of the record of the case. Most court requirements are satisfied by orally announcing the agreement in court as the court reporter takes it down as part of the court record. If the agreement is in the form of a stipulation and court rules require that stipulations be written, however, an oral stipulation for the record will not be binding even though settlements need not otherwise be written.

Parties usually obtain a consent judgment by appearing before the judge in chambers and having the judge sign a judgment order prepared for this purpose. State statutes generally define the exact procedure to be followed. Once filed, the consent judgment will appear in the same manner as a judgment rendered after a full trial. A consent judgment binds the parties both as a judgment of the court and as a contractual agreement.

A dismissal with prejudice to any further suit may be used in place of a consent judgment to add finality to a settlement. State procedures may vary, but the procedure is illustrated in Rule 41(a) of the Federal Rules of Civil Procedure, which requires a stipulation signed by all the parties to be filed with the court. The stipulation must state that the action is dismissed with prejudice or it is assumed to be without prejudice.

6. REQUIRED COURT NOTIFICATION OF SETTLEMENT

Some courts require lawyers to notify the court promptly when a pending action has been settled. Although the settlement is still binding if the lawyers fail to notify the court promptly, in some jurisdictions (such as California) sanctions may be imposed against the lawyers for interfering with court proceedings.

7. COURT APPROVAL OF SETTLEMENTS

The court may be involved in settlement in two ways, which may provide some degree of protection. First, the court may participate in the settlement process. Second, the court may review settlements effected without court supervision. Court participation in the mechanics often begins in pretrial and settlement conferences. Court rules set up the framework for pretrial procedures. For example, Rule 16(a) of the Federal Rules of Civil Procedure states that one of the objectives of a pretrial conference is "facilitating the settlement of the case." Federal Rule 16(c)(7) specifically provides that one of the subjects to be discussed at pretrial conferences is "the possibility of settlement or the use of extrajudicial procedures to resolve the dispute." Other court rules permit discussion of settlement by allowing consideration of any matters which may aid in the disposition of the case. Some states also provide a separate procedure for settlement conferences. Local rules may further modify and clarify the place of settlement discussion in pretrial conference.

Although a judge can encourage settlement in a pretrial conference, the judge may not coerce the parties to settle. For example, in *Kothe v. Smith* (1985), at a pretrial conference three weeks before trial in a malpractice action, the district court judge ordered counsel to conduct settlement negotiations. The judge recommended a settlement between $20,000 and $30,000 and threatened sanctions if the case were settled for a comparable figure after the commencement of the trial. Plaintiff's counsel indicated to the judge that the plaintiff would accept $20,000 but requested the judge not to disclose the figure to the defendant's counsel. The lowest communicated demand was $50,000 and the highest pretrial offer was $5,000. After one day of trial, the case settled for $20,000. Pursuant to Rule 16(f) of the Federal Rules of Civil Procedure, which permits sanctions for failure to comply with pretrial conference orders, the district court judge awarded $2,400 in sanctions against the defendant.

The Second Circuit Court of Appeals reversed the award of sanctions. The court held that the district court's imposition of a penalty against the defendant was an abuse of discretion. The court noted the policy favoring settlements but concluded that the pressure tactics used by the district judge were not permissible. According to the court, Rule 16 is not a means for "clubbing the parties into an involuntary compromise." The court also found the imposition of the sanctions only on the defendant "especially troublesome." Settlement is a two-way street and the defendant had no indication that the plaintiff was willing to accept $20,000 until the conclusion of the first day of trial. Furthermore, sanctions were inappropriate after the trial began because it is not unusual for a defendant to change its evaluation of a case after seeing the plaintiff's performance on the witness stand.

Some settlements, particularly those involving class actions, require court approval. For example, Rule 23(e) of the Federal Rules of Civil Procedure requires court approval before a class action in federal court can be dismissed or compromised. The purpose of court approval is to protect the nonparty class members from unjust or unfair settlements. The underlying concern is that the class representatives may have become fainthearted or been able to secure satisfaction of their claims to the detriment of the nonparty class members. Court approval is also often required for settlements involving the legal claims of minors.

E. INTERPRETING THE SETTLEMENT

Interpretation of settlement agreements is generally limited to the terms of the agreement itself. Extrinsic evidence is generally admissible to show that the agreement is not integrated, the recital of facts is not accurate, the conditions precedent have not been fulfilled, the conditions subsequent have or have not occurred, the agreement was intended to affect third parties, or the stated consideration was never received. Extrinsic evidence may also be used to show that the agreement purports to release the claims of a minor or in some other way violates public policy.

The intent of the parties will generally determine which claims are released when the agreement contains general language. That intent may be judged from both the language of the agreement and the circumstances surrounding its making. Usually, general language is limited by specific language. If the general language indicates that the dominant purpose was a general release, however, it may control. All claims may be released if specific claims are not mentioned because claims arising from a single cause of action cannot be made the subject of separate suits; thus, when the suit as a unit is released, all claims are usually implicitly included.

Often, a party will wish to release a personal injury claim, but not the related property damage claim. Under these circumstances, the property damage claim should be specifically excluded from the settlement agreement. If separate consideration is stated for the release of general and specific claims, effect will be given to the general release.

In general, the principles of contract law apply to settlement agreements and releases. Like other contracts, compromise agreements are formed by a valid offer and acceptance. The acceptance must be within a reasonable time on the terms offered. Acceptance may be implied, such as through retention of an amount tendered in full settlement of the obligation or through the retention of a check or draft. Forbearance from bringing suit, however, does not in itself constitute an offer or an acceptance of compromise—unless it is communicated to the other party as such.

The rules regarding consideration also apply unchanged to settlement agreements. Consideration for the agreement is found in the compromise of amounts demanded and in the relinquishment of claims in a dispute. A subsequent finding that no legal claim was present does not invalidate a compromise if the parties believed in good faith that a valid claim existed.

Ordinarily, the conflict-of-laws principles governing contracts generally are applied to settlements. Thus, the law of the state in which the compromise agreement was made will generally govern questions of validity and construction of the compromise. Questions of authority may be governed by the law of the state in which a party was domiciled or the agency contract was created, and matters relating to the breach of a compromise agreement are generally governed by the law of the state in which the agreement was to be performed.

Because a compromise may have a significant effect on the antecedent obligations of the parties, certain aspects may be governed by the law of the state where those obligations were created, especially in the settlement of tort claims. In tort situations, the law of the place where the tort occurred may be applied.

F. FAIRNESS IN NEGOTIATION RESULTS

Self-Test 4 in Chapter 1(G) raised basic questions about how unfairness in negotiation results should be handled. In answering these questions, lawyers must take into account more than personal predilections. As professionals, lawyers are bound by the current ethical rules and the law itself. To what extent do these sources impose an obligation to be fair and to take into account broader social, judicial, and economic interests in legal negotiation? Can lawyers depend on professional ethical norms to impose an obligation to be "fair"?

The ABA's *Model Code* and the ABA's *Model Rules* support a variety of views of acceptable goals in negotiation. Neither of these sources resolves the conflict between the interest in achieving the best possible outcome and the possibility that, in objective terms, the settlement may be "unfair" to one of the parties. In other words, it is widely regarded that legal negotiators cannot depend on the *minimum* standards of professional ethics to restrain parties from trying to achieve the best settlement possible, though "unfair" to one of the parties.

Many lawyers, of course, would readily accept the proposition suggested by Judge Alvin Rubin in his insightful article, *A Causerie on Lawyers' Ethics in Negotiation*: there is some point beyond which an ethical lawyer may not accept an arrangement that is "completely unfair" or "unconscionable" to the other side—whether it results from vast differences in bargaining power or bargaining skills. The harm imposed at some point represents too great "a sacrifice of value" or the deal becomes "too good to be true" and thus "a cheat." The problem from a negotiator's perspective is that other negotiators may draw the line at different points and in their own minds maintain that the professional ethical rules have not been violated.

The law itself does provide some limitations on unfair negotiated transactions or settlements. However, as Professor Williams points out, the law will help only in the extreme cases. Under the law, the route to setting aside extremely unfair agreements or settlements generally centers on the means used for achieving the unfair outcome, such as coercion, improper threats, misrepresentation, or fraud.

A notable exception, which focuses on objective results rather than means, is the long-standing "lesion beyond moiety" doctrine embodied in Articles 2589-2600 in the *Louisiana Civil Code*: a sale of land ("an immovable estate") may be rescinded if the seller has been "aggrieved for more than one half" of its fair market value at the time of the sale or the granting of an option to purchase, regardless of the circumstances.

Absent the use of improper means to induce opposing lawyers and their clients to agree to terms that are unfair or harmful yet within the bounds of law, the principal question becomes one of morality. In a business context, the issue of business sense also arises. Does the client want to be a part of a transaction that is likely to bring about further difficulties or poor performance? A widespread view of conventional business wisdom suggests that if the contract is not good for both parties, it is not good for either one.

In such circumstances, the course of action left open to legal negotiators by the rules of professional ethics is to consult with their clients and express their misgivings about the moral or practical aspects of the proposed contract or settlement. If a negotiator has strong personal feelings about the matter, the generally accepted view is that the negotiator may withdraw from representing the client, provided withdrawal does not harm the client's interests.

However, the negotiator may not permissibly undermine or openly protest the agreement. In other words, the choice for the lawyer is a personal one. If the client is *legally entitled* to insist on concluding what the lawyer regards to be an "unfair" deal, the lawyer is not free to sabotage the arrangement. On the other hand, the lawyer may withdraw if it can be done without harming the client's interests.

G. DEFECTS IN COMPROMISE AND SETTLEMENT AGREEMENTS

When the validity of settlement agreements is challenged, courts routinely assert a general policy in favor of negotiated settlements. Courts consistently affirm that there is an overriding public interest in settling and quieting litigation, and that it has always been the policy of the law to favor compromise and settlement. This policy is based on the perceived benefits of settlement in comparison with litigation. Settlements reduce legal expenses, save time for the parties and the court, and are more conducive to amicable outcomes and future relations between the parties.

In support of this policy, courts will often enforce settlement agreements despite minor errors in their formation and give broad interpretation to legal rules in order to preserve a settlement. Nonetheless, the policy of favoring settlement agreements is weighed against other considerations of public policy as well. Courts will overturn settlement agreements found contrary to other public interests. Fraud, misrepresentation, and mistake are the most common grounds for invalidating settlement agreements, especially those made by insurance carriers in settlement of tort claims. When injured parties are wrongly induced to settle for much less than the cost of the damages incurred, public policy demands that the settlement be reviewed and possibly rescinded.

Furthermore, a settlement agreement is considered a contract and its validity may be challenged on other traditional contract grounds, including illegality, duress, undue influence, uncertainty or vagueness, lack of capacity or authority, and public policy. The defect, however, must relate to the compromise agreement—not to the antecedent claim.

One special area of concern involves joint tortfeasors, contribution, and so-called Mary Carter Agreements. Joint tortfeasor problems begin with the common-law rule that the release of one joint tortfeasor releases all of the tortfeasors. This rule was based on the rationale that a person is entitled to only one satisfaction on a claim, and satisfaction by one tortfeasor releases all others. This rule stimulated the development of the covenant not to sue. In such a covenant, the injured party makes a contract with the tortfeasor not to bring any action against him in return for the settlement payment. Because no formal release has been given, courts often hold that covenants not to sue do not operate to release the other tortfeasors.

The Uniform Contribution Among Tortfeasors Act abolished the common-law rule of releases and allowed contribution among tortfeasors. In states adopting this act, a release of one tortfeasor does not release the other common tortfeasors. The amount recoverable from the remaining defendants is, however, reduced by the settling defendant's pro rata share of liability so that only one actual satisfaction is received.

A particularly troublesome problem is presented in situations involving a single plaintiff and multiple defendants when one or more of the defendants agrees to settle with the plaintiff for a guaranteed amount, which decreases in an inverse relation to the amount the plaintiff recovers from the remaining defendants. There are many variations of this standard form, but the plaintiff is always guaranteed a specific amount (often given to the plaintiff as an advance), and the defendant's liability is expressly limited.

These settlements, known variously as Guaranteed Verdict Agreements, Mary Carter agreements (after the case of *Booth v. Mary Carter Paint Co.* (1967)) or Gallagher covenants (after *City of Tucson v. Gallagher* (1972)), cause problems. Often the defendants remain a part of the action until the case is over, while their interests have shifted from limiting the plaintiff's recovery to increasing it. Because of the potential for abuse, scholars have strongly opposed these agreements and many states have declared them void as against public policy. All courts have at least required some degree of disclosure to the jury of any such agreements. Some courts, however, have limited the usefulness of the disclosure requirement by allowing information damaging to the remaining defendants to be included in the agreement itself, therefore allowing it to come to the attention of the jury if the pact is revealed.

An example of such an agreement occurred in *General Motors Corp. v. Lahocki* (1980). The plaintiff broke his back when the GM van in which he was riding hit unlit wooden barricades placed in the roadway by defendant Contee Sand and Gravel, Inc. Lahocki was thrown onto the street, suffering a fractured spine. Lahocki sued Contee and GM for negligence, alleging against GM that the vehicle was "uncrashworthy." Before trial Contee and Lahocki made an agreement which provided that Contee would pay to Lahocki $150,000 except (1) if Contee's pro rata share of a judgment against it was in excess of $150,000 then Contee would pay this up to $250,000; (2) if final judgment was entered against GM alone, then Contee would pay nothing to Lahocki, even if Lahocki and GM thereafter settled the case; or (3) if Lahocki settled with GM, then the sum to be paid by Contee to Lahocki was to be $100,000.

This agreement limited Contee's liability to a possible $250,000. If GM were found solely liable or if GM were to settle with Lahocki, then Contee would owe nothing—making it to Contee's advantage to prove GM solely liable. If GM were found not to have been liable, Contee would owe $150,000. The judge was informed of the agreement, but the jury was not. Because of this agreement, the position of Contee in the adversarial proceeding was reversed, and Contee was financially encouraged to assist the plaintiff, unknown to the jury. Therefore, Contee assisted Lahocki in paying the fee of an expert testifying against GM. Since Contee was still appearing as a defendant, his lawyer was allowed to cross-examine Lahocki's witnesses. In doing so Contee's lawyer merely had the witness repeat damaging information against GM and cure defects that Lahocki's lawyer had left. Not realizing Contee's change in position, the jury found GM solely liable and awarded Lahocki $1.2 million (plus $300,000 to his wife).

The court of appeals reversed, and following the trend in some states, held that these agreements are not against public policy per se, but that they must be revealed to the jury so it can evaluate the circumstances.

H. FINAL DISBURSEMENTS

When settlement has been reached with the opposing party, a lawyer should take extra care in explaining the final disbursement of the proceeds of the settlement. Even when these matters have been explained and are contained in the signed representation agreement (as they should have been), the client may need to be reminded again about the fee arrangement and deduction of costs.

I. POST-NEGOTIATION SELF-ANALYSIS

One way to learn from negotiating experiences is to engage in a post-negotiation "self-analysis." For example, in *A Practical Guide to Negotiation*, Thomas F. Guernsey provides a series of excellent self-analysis questions, including:

● "Did you accomplish your goals? Why or why not?"

● "Were you able to set the tone that you desired for the negotiation? Why or why not?"

● "Did you control the agenda? Why or why not?"

● "Did you find [out] as much information as you wanted? Why or why not?"

- "Did you reveal too much information? Why or why not?"
- "Did you fail to reveal information you should have? Why or why not?"
- "If you did not agree, was it appropriate given the context of this particular negotiation? Why or why not?"
- "If you have deadlocked, what might you be able to do to break that deadlock? Why or why not?"
- "What is the one thing you would do differently in the negotiation? Why?"

J. CONCLUSION

You have now seen an overview of the negotiation process from beginning to end. As it is often said, negotiation is certainly not a science—it is an "art." Yet one's "art" can be improved by recognizing the materials that you have to work with, the choices that must be made, and the patterns that are possible.

You have also seen that there are basic strategy and style choices. Good legal negotiators make those choices consciously. So when you are involved in legal negotiation, start with thorough preparation. Decide on a strategy and style, but be flexible. This preparation leads to confidence.

Be keenly observant of what is happening during a legal negotiation. Analyze from the beginning what strategy and style the other side is using. Maintain a high standard of ethical behavior. Be trustworthy and honest. Use questions. Be creative, versatile, and adaptable. Reevaluate your client's priorities and needs as the negotiation process progresses over time. Use new information to reassess your client's BATNA. During all this time, work with your client. Above all, learn from your experience.

*

INDEX

References are to pages

267

BEST ALTERNATIVE TO A NEGOTIATED AGREEMENT ("BATNA")

Adjustment during argumentation stage, 104, 121, 265
Benefits of using, 79
Description of, to client, 78
Defined, 78
"Post-settlement settlement," role in, 249
Realistic expectations, role in developing, 149
Reassessment, 265
Researching to improve negotiating power, 121
Transactional settings, 78

"BLENDED" STYLE

See also Competitive Style; Cooperative Style; Strategy
Described, 69

BLUFFS

Escalation, use of bluff as part of, 245
Illustrations of, 212
Ineffective negotiators, characteristic of, 54, 65, 69, 231
Limits on, 207
Purpose of, 212
Risks, 71, 213, 227, 230
Time pressure, effect on making, 234

BRAINSTORMING

See also Bridging Solutions or Proposals; Closure; Problem-Solving Strategy
During negotiation, 103
Means of inventing options, 116

BREAKS IN NEGOTIATION

Being the "guest" facilitates, 159
Defensive use, 229
Energy cycles of negotiators, 165
Informal discussions during formal negotiations, 104, 192
Normal part of negotiation process, 104, 228
Offensive use, 229

BREAKS IN NEGOTIATION—Cont'd

BRIDGING SOLUTIONS OR PROPOSALS

CALIFORNIA RULES OF PROFESSIONAL CONDUCT

CASE EVALUATION

COMMUNICATION
See also Active Listening; Questions
Active communication with opposing counsel, 166
During litigation, 166
During negotiation, 104, 190
Casual conversation, 192
"Closed" problem-solving situations, 176
Critical element in negotiating, 4
"Game playing" forms of communication
Avoiding, 183
"Boredom," 185
Breaking out of "game playing" patterns, 186
"Expertise," 184
"Funny money," 186
"Impossible client," 185
"Outrageous behavior," 185
Recognizing, 184
"Red herring," 186
"Snow job," 184
"So what," 186
"Wooden leg," 185
"Yes, but," 185, 194
Influencing expectations, 190
Keeping client informed, 12, 203
Non-verbal communication, 200
False non-verbal signals, 201
Part of "boredom" game, 185
Offers, 198
False signals from pattern of, 200
"Leakage" indicating lack of commitment, 100
Reacting to offers, 202
"Rules" for communicating, 198
Slips of the tongue, 199
Pivotal words or phrases, 194
Poor communication, effects of, 191
Promises, communicating, 226
Questions during negotiating sessions, 124
Planning, 123

COMMUNICATION—Cont'd

COMPETENCE

COMPETITIVE STYLE

LOSS OF NEGOTIATING CURRENCY
See Currency (Negotiating)

LOSS OF POSITION
See Position Loss

LOUISIANA CIVIL CODE
Articles 2589-2600 (lesion beyond moiety), 257

MALPRACTICE
Failure to make authorized offer, 152
Lack of negotiating skill, 6, 10
Negligently recommending settlement, 19
Professional relationship, effect of, 7
Recommending unreasonable settlement offer, 12

MARY CARTER AGREEMENTS
See Settlement

MEDIATION
Business disputes, resolving through, 107
Dispute resolution clauses, 113
Effect of widespread training on legal negotiation, 71
Helping to justify and reinforce the agreement, 246
Presence of mediator increasing pressure toward agreement, 169
Reopening stalled negotiations, 229
Single negotiating text, 172

MEDICAL EXPENSES, OFFERS TO PAY
See Evidence

MINIMUM DISPOSITION
See also Bargaining Range; Resistance Points; Target
Points
Adjustment during argumentation stage, 102
Danger of setting, 79
Defined, 74
Hiding, 97, 175

MODEL RULES OF PROFESSIONAL CONDUCT—Cont'd

NEGOTIATION NOTEBOOKS

NEW YORK PENAL LAW

"NIBBLING"

NON-VERBAL COMMUNICATION

NOTES

NUMBER OF NEGOTIATORS

OBJECTIVE CRITERIA

OBJECTIVE STANDARDS

PRIVILEGED EXCEPTION THEORY
See Evidence

PROBLEM-SOLVING STRATEGY
See also Adversarial Strategy; Competitive Style;
    Cooperative Style; Information; Initial Proposals
Alternatives, discovering and evaluating, 79, 81, 84, 100, 105,
    242
Areas for potential mutual gain, 85
    Focus on underlying use of money to encourage problem
        solving, 86
Brainstorming, 103, 116
Bridging solutions, see Bridging Solutions or Proposals
"Closed" situations, 176
Combinations of styles and strategies, 87
Dual concerns model, 91
Examples, 79, 80, 83, 84
Idea opponents, 219
Information gathering, 103
    Use of "why" questions, 103, 176
Information giving, 103
Listening, 103, 176
    See also Active Listening
Logrolling, see Closure
Non-zero-sum games, 83, 100
Opening the negotiation, 176
Options, inventing, 116
Personal injury cases, application to, 79
Questions following proposals, 103, 176
"True" problem solvers, 88, 90
Underlying interests and needs, 79, 81, 191
    Probing during argumentation stage, 103

**PROCEDURAL RULES AFFECTING OFFERS OF
    COMPROMISE**
See Federal Rules of Civil Procedure

PROMISES

Bribes, 227

Communicating, 226

Dealing with irritating, ineffective competitive negotiators, 232

Free concession of promising to cooperate, 166

Threats, "flip-side" relationship to, 226

PSYCHOLOGICAL ASPECTS OF NEGOTIATION

Audiences, effect of, 168

"Battle fatigue," 246

"Buyer's remorse," 246

Competitive style, moving psychologically toward other
    negotiator, 55, 62, 214

Cooperative style, moving psychologically toward other
    negotiator, 55, 57, 179

"Costs," 2

Divorce and domestic relations, high psychological involvement,
    28

Harm, 9

Healing process, 3

Labor disputes, "psychological warfare" in, 24

Likelihood of a favorable verdict, psychological factors, 143

Location of negotiation, psychological aspects of, 158

Midpoint, natural tendency to settle toward, 98, 174

Needs of the parties, in terms of, 82, 176

"Nibbling," role of psychology in, 243

Physical setting, psychological aspects of, 160

Potential losses "loom larger" than equivalent gains, 121

Seating, 160, 163

Stages of negotiation, 94, 106

PUBLICITY

See Ground Rules

PUFFING PRIVILEGE

See Misrepresentation

SETTLEMENT—Cont'd
Guaranteed verdict agreements, 261
Healing process, part of, 3
Institutional significance, 3, 26
Interpreting the settlement, 254
Judge, role of, 251
Lawyer's economic interest, 3
Mary Carter agreements, 261
Offers, see Offers
    As evidence, see Evidence
    Shifting costs, see Federal Rules of Civil Procedure
"Post-settlement settlement," 249
Proof of, 249
Rates, 1, 68, 100
Releases, 254
Structured settlements, 80
    Professional economic analysis, 148
    Software programs, 149
    Taxation of, 139
Time in practice spent on in terms of percent, 2

SHARE-BARGAINING
See Distributive Bargaining

SILENCE
Cultural differences in tolerating, 202
Inducing gap filling, 171, 202
Intimidation, sidestepping, using, 217
Tactic, after an offer has been made, 202

SINGLE NEGOTIATING TEXT
Advantages and disadvantages, 172
Prepared by mediator, 172

SITE
See Location

TRUST
See also Cooperation Facilitators
Adversarial approach, effect of, 21
Communication isolation, promoting distrust, 191
Effective legal negotiators, trustworthy characteristic of, 53
Equitable positioners, 99
Game playing, promoting distrust, 184
Ineffective competitive negotiators, 64
Intimidation, creating mistrust, 67, 216
Maintaining reputation as trustworthy, 214
Orientation stage, developing, 96
Prisoner's Dilemma, 83, 84
Restraint on parties when trust lacking, 2
Stretching facts of case, 212
Trustful, warning sign in terms of effectiveness, 54, 59
Trusting atmosphere, 57, 179
    Lack of reciprocal cooperation, 99
Trustworthy, characteristic of effective negotiators, 53

TRUTH IN LEGAL NEGOTIATIONS
See also Misrepresentation; Trust
Bluffs, 212
Exaggeration, 62, 214
False issues, 63, 182
Generally, 206
Hypothetical situations, 209
Legal safeguards, 222
Maintaining reputation as trustworthy, 214
Professional safeguards against dishonesty, 206, 207
Protecting information, 195
Puffing, 209
Stretching facts of case, 212
"To tell the truth," 194

TRUTH IN LENDING
See Federal Truth in Lending Act

"WINCE"
As a tactic, 202

WRAP-UP DETAILS
See Stages of Negotiation

ZERO-SUM
See Distributive Bargaining

†